Adobe®

Adobe

Photoshop CS

CREATIVE STUDIO

Techniques for Digital Artists

Luanne Seymour Cohen

Adobe Photoshop CS Creative Studio, Techniques for Digital Artists
by Luanne Seymour Cohen

Copyright © 2004 by Luanne Seymour Cohen

This Adobe Press book is published by Peachpit Press.

For information on Adobe Press books, contact:

Peachpit Press

1249 Eighth Street

Berkeley, CA 94710

510/524-2178 (tel) / 510/524-2221 (fax)

To report errors, please send a note to errata@peachpit.com

Peachpit Press is a division of Pearson Education

For the latest on Adobe Press books, go to http://www.adobe.com/adobepress

Editor: Becky Morgan

Production Coordinator: Lisa Brazieal

Copyeditor: Judy Walthers von Alten

Book design: Jan Martí, Command Z

Cover design: Aren Howell

ISBN 0-321-22043-9

9 8 7 6 5 4 3 2 1

Printed and bound in the United States of America

Acknowledgments

"Break a leg!" is what they say before you go on stage for a big performance. My big performance last summer was to write this book, so while taking digital pictures at Point Lobos, California (on the Monterey Peninsula), I fractured my leg. My family and friends rushed to my aid. I could not have finished this book without their help. My husband and son cut their vacation short. My daughter shopped for me. My father and stepmother drove me around town. My aunt waited on me and nursed me back to health. My mother cooked for me. Many of my friends brought me dinners, flowers, cards, and gifts.

It is only fitting that I use this page to thank these wonderful people who really helped me during this time of great need. Thank you very much for all your help and support: Rick, Jessica, and Charlie Cohen; Paula Horn, Margo and Dale Seymour, Steven Ready, Gay and Chelsea Allen, Linda and Chic Bales, Sue and Bruce Arnold, Leslie and John Cutler, Dr. Stephen Osborn, Rachel Barnett, and the women in my fiber arts group.

I would also like to thank the people who have worked on this book with me. I couldn't have picked a better team: Judy Walthers von Alten, Jan Marti, Becky Morgan, and Lisa Brazieal.

Thanks, everyone. And when they tell you, "Break a leg!"—don't take them literally.

About the author

Luanne Seymour Cohen has been a graphic designer for the last 27 years. Some of the Silicon Valley companies she has worked for include Atari, Apple Computer, and Adobe Systems. She was a Creative Director at Adobe for 12 years where she created package designs and illustrations, and produced a variety of collateral materials for Adobe and its software products. She also developed and designed the Adobe Collector's Edition products. Her responsibilities included working closely with the engineers as an advisor during the development of Adobe's graphic software. She wrote and illustrated four editions of *Design Essentials* and another book in the series, *Imaging Essentials*. She has also written several books in the Adobe Press *Classroom in a Book* series.

Some of her award-winning work has been shown in Communication Arts, Print magazine, the Type Directors Club, Print casebooks, and the AIGA annual. She has taught workshops and classes all over the world, including at Stanford University, Kent State University, University of California at Santa Barbara, Anderson Ranch Arts Center, Center for Creative Imaging, the Thunder Lizard Photoshop and Illustrator conferences, and California College of Arts and Crafts. An avid quilter for many years, she has taught classes and written articles on digital quilt and fabric design. Under her father's imprint in 1995, she published a book, *Quilt Design Masters* (Dale Seymour Publications/Addison Wesley), that is used in elementary school classrooms to teach mathematical principles. She lives and teaches in the San Francisco Bay Area.

Contents

Introduction

Adobe Photoshop CS Creative Studio shows how to produce traditional graphic and photographic effects using Adobe Photoshop CS software. This book does not attempt to describe all the features of the software program. Instead it is a quick, how-to recipe book for artists familiar with the basic tools and commands in the programs.

Each technique has been tested by professional designers, Web page designers, illustrators, teachers, photographers, and novice users. Even though I make the assumption that the reader has a basic working knowledge of the software, I have included an appendix that reviews the basic shortcuts and commands that I use every day with these programs. Most of the pages include tips and shortcut sidebars. Some are general tips that can be used with any technique. Some are specific additions or variations of the technique on that page.

Adobe Photoshop CS Creative Studio covers the most recent version of the software for both Macintosh and Windows platforms: Adobe Photoshop CS and Adobe Illustrator CS. Many, but not all, of these techniques can be used with older versions of the software. Look for the platform-specific shortcuts in the appendix. When keys are indicated in the text, I use a slash (/) to separate the Macintosh and Windows key needed. For example:

"Press Option/Alt when clicking a button" means

Mac OS X users press the Option key.

Windows users press the Alt key.

Unless mentioned otherwise, all files used in these techniques are in RGB color mode.

Working efficiently

Using layer comps

When working with different design ideas, layer comps can be extremely useful. You can take snapshots of different Layers palette states and have the snapshots saved with the file. What can be saved in a layer comp is limited. The only changes that will be recorded are layer visibility, position, or appearance. Layer comps are most useful when combining images, type, or both in different relationships.

To create a layer comp, choose Window > Layer Comps and click the New Layer Comp button at the bottom of the Layer Comps palette.

This book is full of tips and shortcuts to make working with Photoshop quicker and easier. Before you dive into the techniques, here are some basic tips about how to work more efficiently while using Photoshop. This is by no means an exhaustive guide on how to use each feature mentioned. For more information on the features or tools discussed here, see the Photoshop CS user guide or Photoshop Help.

Setting up your workspace

Save different workspaces—Once you set up your workspace for a project, you can save and reuse the setup. For example, if you are working on a digital painting, you may want to have only the Brushes and Layers palettes and the toolbox visible. To save a workspace, close all unneeded palettes and position the open palettes the way you want them. Choose Window > Workspace > Save Workspace. To reset the palettes to their default positions, choose Window > Workspace > Reset Palette Locations. Make and save workspaces for the different types of projects you create. To use a workspace that you've saved, choose Window > Workspace > and then choose the name of the workspace from the bottom of the menu.

Dock palettes in the palette well—If your screen space is tight, dock some of the palettes in the palette well in the tool options bar. The palette well is the long rectangular area on the right side of the tool options bar. To dock a palette, drag the palette tab up to the well and release the mouse button. To display a palette in the palette well, click the tab. To remove a palette from the well, drag the palette tab out of the well and release the mouse button.

Dock palettes together—You can also save space by docking your palettes together. To dock a palette with another palette, drag the tab of the palette onto the second palette. When the target palette becomes highlighted, release the mouse button. The palette will adapt to the size of the target palette.

Using the File Browser to organize your images

Learn how to use the features in the File Browser—The effort will pay off by saving you lots of time as you work on projects in Photoshop CS. The File Browser is a very efficient way to organize and access your image files. You can sort the files several different ways.

Flag files for easy viewing and selecting—If you've just downloaded a batch of images from your digital camera, you'll want to go through them and flag the ones you want to use. Once the files are flagged, you can sort them by choosing Sort > Flag from the File Browser menu. The flagged files are then placed at the beginning of the group in the File Browser window. You can also view only the flagged files to save searching time. Choose View > Flagged Files from the File Browser menu.

Use keywords to speed up image searches—Add keywords to your files to make searching for them easy. For example, say you took 36 photographs at the beach with your digital camera. Open up the folder in the File Browser, select the image thumbnails that contain a common subject, and add keywords to all of them at once. In this example, you might add the word "Poison Oak." You can also select individual files and add other keywords such as subject matter, dominant colors, or people's names. Spending a little time adding keywords will be a great help when you are in a rush looking for a certain image and can't remember the file name.

To search for a file using a keyword, click the Search button at the top of the File Browser window. Select Keywords as the

Using layer styles

Layer styles let you add many different effects to a layer, such as drop shadows, strokes, patterns, or bevel and emboss.

- **Create and save your own layer styles**— Once created, layer styles can be reopened at any time and changed. You can also copy and paste them onto another layer, saving you the time of recreating them. To save layer styles as a preset for use in other files, select the layer in the Layers palette that contains the style you want to save. Choose Window > Styles to display the Styles palette. Click the New Style button at the bottom of the Styles palette. Name the style and click OK.

- **Use preset layer styles**— Select a layer in the Layers palette. Display the Style palette and choose a preset style from the Style palette by clicking its thumbnail. You can choose from a library of saved presets by displaying the pop-up menu in the Styles palette and choosing one of the library files at the bottom of the menu. The styles will be added to the palette thumbnails. Click a style to apply it to the selected layer.

Using layers for maximum flexibility

Try to use layers as often as possible. They let you edit and change the image without having to redo or undo hours of work. When using layers, try to use these Layers palette features:

• **Layer sets**—Keep your files organized and easy to edit by using layer sets. For example, if you are doing an illustration of a group of animals, you might devote one layer set to each animal.

• **Adjustment layers**— Adjustment layers can save you lots of time because they are editable. You can turn them on and off or change the settings at any time.

• **Layer masks**—When you want to isolate part of a layer, use a layer mask instead of making a selection and deleting pixels. You never know when you might need those pixels. Layer masks can be edited and turned on or off at any time.

Criteria, enter the keyword you are searching for, and click Search. The images that contain that keyword will appear in the window.

Search for keywords

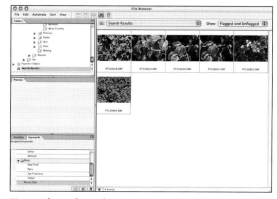

Keyword search results

Using keyboard shortcuts

Use the keyboard to quickly change tools—Each tool in the toolbox has a letter shortcut assigned to it: just type the letter and the tool changes. To view the shortcuts, position the pointer over a tool in the toolbox. When the tooltip appears, the shortcut letter will appear next to the tool name. You can also find the tool shortcuts in Photoshop Help.

Use the keyboard to access menu items—Many of the menu commands have keyboard shortcuts. To view the shortcuts, choose a menu. The shortcut is displayed to the right of the command name. For a list of many of the shortcuts, see "Appendix A: Shortcuts" on page 314 or see Photoshop Help.

Using presets

Create your own presets—If you have certain settings that you use repeatedly, create presets for them. For example, this book has several illustration sizes. To save time, presets were created for each illustration size. When a new file was created, the preset size was chosen from the Preset pop-up menu in the New dialog box.

You can also create presets for tools. To save a tool preset, select the tool and enter the settings in the tool options bar. Choose Window > Tool Presets to display the Tool Preset palette; then choose Save Tool Presets from the palette pop-up menu.

Using the History palette

Make snapshots as you work—When you are painting or exploring filter effects, it's a good idea to capture image states as you go along. That way, you can go back to a specific state if you find you've gone too far with a certain technique. Take snapshots by choosing New Snapshot from the History palette pop-up menu. Choose one of the options from the From menu in the New Snapshot dialog box and click OK.

Remember that the snapshots exist only until you close the file or quit Photoshop. If you want to save a particular state as a separate file, select that state in the History palette. Then click the New Document From Current State button at the bottom of the History palette. Save the file.

Using actions for repeated tasks

Use actions in the Actions palette menu—Choose an action from the action sets at the bottom of the Actions palette menu.

Make your own actions—Make an action by recording a series of commands that you use frequently. For instructions on how to record an action, see the Photoshop CS user guide or Photoshop Help.

Efficiently selecting

When faced with selecting a large or complicated object, try one of these ideas:

- **Look at the Channels palette**—Often, the object you are selecting can be more easily isolated by duplicating one of the channels. For example, if you want to select a red rose on a background of green leaves, look at the Red channel. The rose will look almost white. Duplicate that channel by dragging it onto the New Channel button at the bottom of the Channels palette. You've already got a head start on a selection. Now use a combination of selection tools and adjustment commands to finish creating the rose selection channel.

- **Combine tools**—The magnetic lasso might work on most of the edges of an object but not all. That's okay. Make the selection and then click the Quick Mask button at the bottom of the toolbox. Clean up the selection with the brush tool.

- **Isolate the area before using Color Range**—Use the marquee tools or the lasso tool to make a rough selection around the object you want to select before using the Color Range command. A rough selection reduces the amount of clean-up work you have to do after applying the Color Range command.

Section 1 Painting

1 Painterly images

Here's a way to turn your photographs into beautiful, textural digital paintings. Photoshop has many built-in filters that produce a painterly or sketchy texture. You'll separate the color from the texture to give you more control over the final effect. Several variations on the basic steps appear at the end of the technique. Just substitute the filter shown in the variation for the one used in step 8, and you'll get a very different result.

1   Open an RGB image. Much of the detail will be lost in this technique, so pick an image with a strong composition and vibrant colors.

The image should start in RGB mode with 8 bits/channel because many of the filters used in this technique work only on 8-bit RGB images.

Open an 8-bit RGB image

2   If your image is strongly colored, you may want to skip this step. To enhance the vibrancy of the colors and the contrast, choose Image > Adjustments > Shadow/Highlights. Increase the percentage of Color Correction and adjust the Highlights and Shadows until your image has slightly

Channel Mixer versus Desaturate

When converting an image from color to black and white, you have several choices. You can choose Image > Adjustments > Desaturate or Channel Mixer. The method that gives you the most control is Channel Mixer. It's also available as an adjustment layer. Desaturate removes the colors but leaves the values the same. Channel Mixer allows you to select the percentage of each channel used to create the grayscale image as you preview the results. Depending on your needs, you can adjust the image to make it more contrasty or to make certain colors stand out.

Original image

Desaturate method

Channel Mixer method

exaggerated colors and tones. Remember, you're turning this into a painting, so you want the colors to be bright.

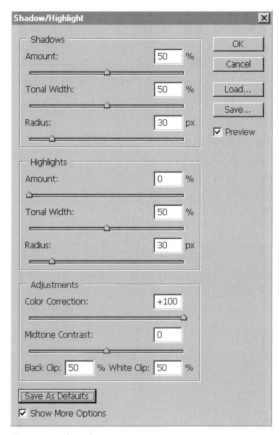

Exaggerate the colors

3   Option/Alt-drag the Background layer thumbnail in the Layers palette onto the New Layer button to duplicate the background. Name this layer Texture. This layer will define only the texture of the final image, not the color.

4   Choose Image > Adjustments > Channel Mixer. Select the Monochrome option to remove the color, and start out with the values in the example. Adjust for your image if necessary.

Using the Channel Mixer command gives you more flexibility than the Desaturate command.

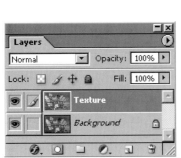

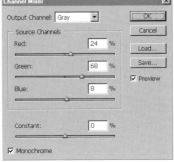

Create the Texture layer   *Desaturate with the Channel Mixer*

Shortcut:
View layers

Click the eye icon in the Layers palette to show or hide a layer. Option/Alt-click the eye icon to show or hide all other visible layers. For example, if you want only the Color layer to show in step 6, Option/Alt-click the eye icon for the Color layer. All the other layers except the Color layer are automatically hidden.

5   Duplicate the Background layer and name it Color. This layer will define the colors of your painting. Drag the Color layer above the Texture layer in the Layers palette.

6   Set the blending mode for the Color layer to Color. Then hide the Background and Texture layers.

The Color mode retains the color from that layer but picks up any texture from the layers beneath it.

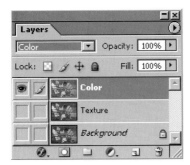

Create the Color layer

7   With the Color layer still selected, choose Filter > Blur > Smart Blur. Experiment with the Radius and Threshold values until the image has a cartoony or airbrushed look. Set the Quality to High, and click OK.

Notice that the details and much of the texture have been blurred away. Don't worry about the loss of details; they will be restored in the next step.

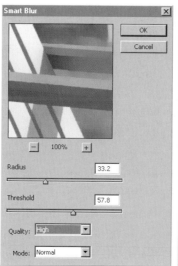

Use Smart Blur on the Color layer

8   Select the Texture layer to make it active and visible.

9   Choose Filter > Artistic > Dry Brush. You will get different texture effects depending on the resolution of your image. Experiment with different values until you are satisfied with the texture. Click OK.

This example of a 300-ppi image used values of Brush Size = 6, Brush Detail = 7, and Texture = 2.

Use a filter to texturize the Texture layer

10 If you are satisfied with the effect, save or print the image. If you want to enhance the colors, continue with the next step.

Evaluate the color and texture

Getting a bigger filter preview

Click the toggle button to the left of the OK button to hide the filter controls in the dialog box and enlarge the image preview area.

11 Select the Color layer in the Layers palette. Click the New Adjustment layer button at the bottom of the Layers palette and choose Hue/Saturation. Adjust the settings until you are satisfied with the effect. Click OK.

In this example, the Saturation value was increased to +41.

Add an adjustment layer above the Color layer

12 If you are satisfied with the effect, save or print the image. To experiment with other textures and effects, try the following variations.

Completed image

Variation: Texturizer

Follow step 1 and then steps 4
through 6; don't create a texture
layer. Choose Filter > Texture >
Texturizer.

Settings:
Texture = Canvas
Scaling = 109%
Relief = 5
Light = Top Left

Variation: Colored Pencil

Press the D key to set the foreground and background colors to
their defaults. Replace step 8 with:
Choose Filter > Artistic > Colored
Pencil.

Settings:
Pencil Width = 4
Stroke Pressure = 12
Paper Brightness = 25

Variation: Spatter

Replace step 8 with:
Choose Filter >
Brush Strokes > Spatter.

Settings:
Spray Radius = 17
Smoothness = 5

Variation: Poster Edges

Replace step 8 with: Choose
Filter > Artistic > Poster Edges.

Settings:
Edge Thickness = 1
Edge Intensity = 1
Posterization = 2

Variation: Rough Pastels

Replace step 8 with: Choose Filter > Artistic > Rough Pastels. Set the Texture layer to 60% opacity.

Settings:
Stroke Length = 12
Stroke Detail = 18
Texture = Canvas
Scaling = 50%
Relief = 29
Light = Left

Variation: Sprayed Strokes

Replace step 8 with: Choose Filter > Brush Strokes > Sprayed Strokes.

Settings:
Stroke Length = 20
Spray Radius = 22
Stroke Direction = Left Diagonal

Variation: Cutout

Replace step 8 with: Choose
Filter > Artistic > Cutout.

Settings:
Number of Levels = 5
Edge Simplicity = 6
Edge Fidelity = 1

Variation: Watercolor

Replace step 8 with: Choose
Filter > Artistic > Watercolor.

Settings:
Brush Detail = 14
Shadow Intensity = 0
Texture = 1

Variation: Pointillize

Replace step 8 with:
Set the background color
to 50% gray. Choose Filter >
Pixelate > Pointillize.

Settings:
Cell Size = 5

Variation: Fresco

Replace step 8 with: Set the
texture layer to 75% opacity and
choose Filter > Artistic > Fresco.

Settings:
Brush Size = 2
Brush Detail = 8
Texture = 1

2 | Outlined images

Transform a flat or dull photograph into a graphic illustration with this technique. Start with an image that has edges that you want to emphasize. The best images for this technique are simple without a lot of contrasty texture. You'll end up with a Color layer that has a softened, airbrushed look to it, and with an Outline layer that overlays the Color layer.

1   Open an image that you want to outline. Use an image of at least 300 dpi, because the outline edges look better. Images that have interesting, clearly defined edges work best.

Open a 300-dpi image

2   Option/Alt-drag the layer you want to outline to the New Layer button at the bottom of the Layers palette to duplicate the layer. Name the layer Color.

The example shows the Background layer duplicated.

3   To intensify the colors, create an adjustment layer by clicking the New Adjustment Layer button at the bottom of the Layers palette and selecting Hue/Saturation.

You'll make the image look more like an illustration by creating a more surreal color scheme.

What are good images for outlining?

Look for contrasty images or images that contain sharp, clear edges around shapes. These images make good subjects for outlining:
• Buildings
• Cars, boats, trains, planes
• Roads, bridges, signs
• Furniture, kitchenware
• Fruits and vegetables
Images that don't usually work well for outlining include:
• Trees with lots of leaves
• Grass, sand, dirt
• Flower groups
• Human faces

Duplicate the image layer

Create a Hue/Saturation adjustment layer

4 Adjust the Hue, Saturation, or Lightness to make your image more dramatic.

Each image will require a different adjustment. You can change an adjustment layer at any time, so if needed, you can make more color changes later.

Make the colors in the image more dramatic

5 Select the Color layer, and choose Filter > Blur > Smart Blur. Set the Quality to High and the Mode to Normal. Start with the Radius and Threshold values shown here, and then adjust them for your image. The goal is to smooth out the inside of the shapes while retaining crisp edges. Click OK.

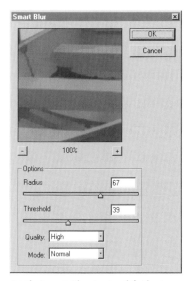

Apply Smart Blur to simplify the image

Shortcut: Quickly open the last-used filter

To apply the last filter you used with the same settings, use the keyboard shortcut of Command/Ctrl+F.

To open the dialog box of the last filter you used, use the keyboard shortcut of Command+Option+F (Mac OS X) or Ctrl+Alt+F (Windows).

6 Evaluate the resulting Color layer. It should be missing much of its original texture. The shapes should be simplified and have well-defined edges. If you are not satisfied with the result, undo, and try step 5 again with different values.

Evaluate the image

7 Option/Alt-drag the Color layer to the New Layer button at the bottom of the Layers palette to duplicate the layer. Name this layer Outline.

Using color outlines instead of black

If you want less black and more color in your outlines, skip step 8. In step 10, set the Outline layer mode to Multiply rather than Darken.

8   Choose Image > Adjustments > Channel Mixer to remove the color from the image. Select Monochrome and use these settings: R = 24, G = 68, and B = 8. Adjust the values if necessary to retain the edge detail in your image. Click OK.

Removing the color before you create the outlines gives you the black edges in step 9.

Create the Outline layer   Remove the color with Channel Mixer

9   Create the outlines by choosing Filter > Stylize > Find Edges.

Use Find Edges on the Outline layer

10 Set the Outline layer mode in the Layers palette to Darken. If you are satisfied with the result, stop here. If the image still needs some finessing, continue with step 11.

Darken applies only the dark edges to the image. The white areas are ignored.

Set the Outline layer to Darken

11 If the outlines are too weak or too thick, correct them with another adjustment layer. Option/Alt-click the New Adjustment Layer button at the bottom of the Layers palette, and select Brightness/Contrast. Select the Group With Previous Layer option. Click OK.

12 Adjust the Brightness/Contrast values until you are satisfied with the outlines. Click OK.

To make the lines darker, reduce the brightness and increase the contrast. To make the lines lighter, increase the brightness and decrease the contrast.

Adjust the outline thickness with Brightness/Contrast

3 | Digital paintings

In just a few simple steps, you can change a run-of-the-mill snapshot or stock photo into a digital painting. Use the brushes available to you in the Brushes palette, or create your own to add texture and a more painterly feel. You'll add texture by creating a Canvas or Paper Texture layer. Then you'll create a pattern out of the image and use the pattern stamp tool to create an impressionistic painting from the original photo.

1   Open a new file. If the file has several layers, flatten them and choose File > Save As to save the file with a new name.

Open a new file

2   If your image has flat or dull colors, intensify them for the painting as needed. Create an adjustment layer by clicking the New Adjustment Layer button at the bottom of the Layers palette. Choose Hue/Saturation. Move the Saturation slider to the right to intensify the colors in your image. Click OK.

Note: You can adjust the image's color saturation and the contrast at the same time by using the Shadow/Highlight command. Choose Image > Adjustments > Shadow/Highlight to open the dialog box. Turn on the Preview option and change

Selecting photos for digital paintings

When selecting a photograph to be turned into a digital painting, look for these qualities:

- Strong, recognizable shapes that will still be recognizable after distortion.
- Bright or strong colors (color-correct or enhance if necessary).
- A strong composition (crop the image, if necessary).
- Good color contrast.

the values until you are satisfied with the result. To adjust the color saturation, change the value with the Color Correction slider. The goal here is to make the image look slightly surreal. Remember, it's going to become a painting, not a photograph; exaggerating the colors in the base image will help it look more painterly.

Intensify the colors with Hue/Saturation or Shadow/Highlight

3   Choose Merge Down from the Layers palette menu to combine the adjustment layer with the image layer. Choose Window > History, and click the New Snapshot button to create a new snapshot of the current state of your image.

Take several snapshots as you make a painting. Snapshots let you go back to a stage that you liked, if needed.

4   Create a new layer in the Layers palette, and name it Paper Texture (or Canvas Texture) depending on the texture you want to use.

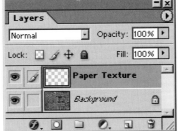

Create a snapshot   *Create the Paper Texture layer*

Shortcut: Fill a selection or layer with white

Press the D key to return the foreground and background colors to their default values of black and white, respectively. Then press Command+Delete (Mac OS X) or Ctrl+Backspace (Windows) to fill with the background color of white.

5   Choose Edit > Fill and fill the Paper or Canvas texture layer with White.

6   Choose Filter > Texture > Texturizer. Choose the Canvas texture, or choose Load Texture from the Texture menu, navigate to Adobe Photoshop CS > Presets > Textures, select the Stucco 2.psd file, and click Open.

Use the example settings or change them to suit your artwork. Look for more textures on your Photoshop CD in the Goodies > Textures for Lighting Effects folder.

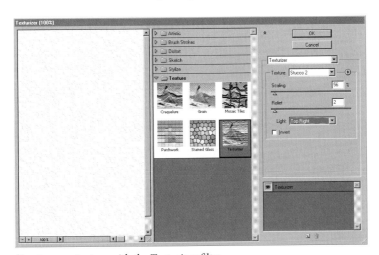

Create paper texture with the Texturizer filter

7   Set the Paper Texture layer blending mode to Multiply. This lets you to see the image through the Paper Texture layer.

Making the paper texture more obvious

With certain images, the Paper Texture layer may be too subtle. If you want that texture to be more pronounced, try this. Drag the Paper Texture layer thumbnail onto the New Layer button in the Layers palette. You now have two Paper Texture layers. Because their mode is set to Multiply, the effect is cumulative. Repeat duplication of the Paper Texture layer if you want the layer texture to be even more pronounced. You can merge the texture layers if desired.

Another method is to create an adjustment layer and group it with the Paper Texture layer. Create either a Levels or Curves adjustment layer. Group it with the Paper Texture layer and adjust the midtone values until you are satisfied with the effect.

8 Click the Background layer in the Layers palette, and Option/Alt-drag the layer onto the New Layer button at the bottom of the palette to duplicate and name it. Name the new layer Painting.

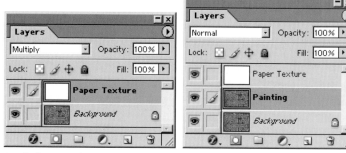

Set the layer mode to Multiply   *Create the Painting layer*

9 Choose Select > All, and then Edit > Define Pattern to create a new pattern tile of the entire image. Name the pattern and click OK.

This pattern will be the image you'll use as the source for your painting.

Select all and define a pattern

10 With the Painting layer still selected, press Delete/Backspace to remove the image from that layer. Choose Select > Deselect.

The layer won't look different because you can still see the Background layer, but you'll see the difference in the Layers palette.

11 Select the pattern stamp tool in the toolbox. Turn on the Impressionist option in the tool options bar. Click the Pattern pop-up palette and select the pattern you created in step 9.

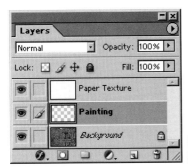

Delete image from the Painting layer   *Set the pattern stamp tool to Impressionist*

12 Select a brush in the Brushes palette, or create a custom brush that matches the texture of the subject matter.

13 Begin painting the image. The Impressionist option samples the colors that are in the snapshot and lets you move them around. Zoom in to paint certain sections or objects in your image.

Pressure-sensitive tablets and the pattern stamp tool

When you use the pattern stamp tool with a pressure-sensitive tablet, you will be able to use the Shape Dynamics feature in the Brushes palette with some of the brushes. But if you select the Impressionist option, the brush diameter will not change with pen pressure.

Creating an underpainting layer

Many painters start by painting a solid color on their canvas before they paint the main image. The solid color serves to unify the composition with bits of color throughout the painting. Often the undercolor is strong and may not occur in the base image. To create an underpainting layer, click the New Adjustment Layer button in the Layers palette and choose Solid Color from the menu. Select a color from the color picker and click OK. Move the Solid Color layer below the Painting layer in the Layers palette. The effect will depend on how densely you painted the Painting layer in steps 13 to 15. In the following examples, compare the shadow areas with an underpainting of white and of purple.

White underpainting layer

Purple underpainting layer

Begin painting the image

14 Continue to paint in the image on the Painting layer. If you want to see the image without the Background layer showing through, turn off the Background layer in the Layers palette. If you want to see a tint of the Background layer, first convert the Background layer to a regular layer (see "About the Background layer" on page 187 for more information); then set its opacity to 50% or less.

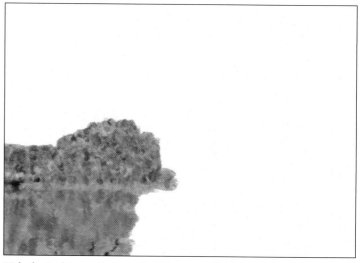

Hide the Background layer to view the paper texture

15 As you paint, change the brush size or brush stroke direction based on the subject matter. Continue painting until the image is complete. You can leave the Background layer turned on or off, according to your taste.

Finish painting the image

Using the correct size paintbrush to retain detail

The size of the paintbrush that you use is critical to the success of your digital painting. Decide how much detail you want to keep. The smaller the brush, the more detail will appear in the painting. The larger the brush, the more generalized the shapes and details will become.

For example, if you are creating a painting of a person's face, you want to retain certain details in the face like the eyes or nostrils. These details may disappear as you paint, for unsatisfactory results (unless you want an abstract look).

Brush = Twice size of one red flower   *Brush = Size of one red flower*

4 Marbled paper

The Italian art of marbleizing is difficult and messy, but it produces some really lovely papers and fabrics. With Photoshop's Liquify filter, you can make your own digital marbled paper without the oily paints and mess. To get the base colors, you'll select a tiny area of any digital image. Then you'll enlarge the selection, blur it, and liquify it. Once you've created several sheets of marbled paper, put them to use in a collage or as backgrounds for pages in a book.

Shortcut: Zoom in quickly

No matter what tool you are using, you can always access the zoom tool from the keyboard. Press Command/Ctrl+spacebar and then drag a marquee around the area you want to enlarge.

Marbled paper

1   Open an RGB image that contains the colors you want to use in your marbling.

The example below is part of a larger photograph of two women in jeans and T-shirts, sitting on the grass.

2   Use the zoom tool to zoom in on the image until you can see the individual pixels. Use the rectangular marquee tool to select an area that contains the colors you want to use.

In this example, the dark jeans and a bit of the green shirt were selected.

Open an RGB image

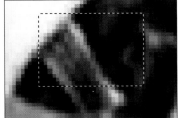
Zoom in and select pixels

3   Choose Edit > Copy to copy the selection. Open a new RGB file. It should be several times larger than the selection you just copied. Choose Edit > Paste. The small selection will be pasted on a layer of its own called Layer 1.

Cancelling and undoing transformations

If you have made a few transformations to a selection but haven't applied them yet, you can still undo the last action by pressing Command/Ctrl+Z. This will only undo the last action performed. For example, if you chose Free Transform and moved the selection and then scaled it, you can undo the scale because it was the last action performed.

To cancel the transformation completely and return to the original selection, do one of the following:
- Press Command/Ctrl+. (period).
- Press Esc.
- Click the Cancel button in the options bar.

4   Choose Photoshop > Preferences > General (Mac OS X) or Edit > Preferences > General (Windows). Change the Image Interpolation to Nearest Neighbor. Click OK.

Nearest Neighbor keeps the pixel colors from blurring together when you scale them. (See "Choosing an Image Interpolation method" on the following page.) You'll scale them in the next step.

 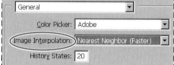

Paste the selection into a new file   *Change the Image Interpolation method*

5   Choose Edit > Free Transform. Enlarge the selection to the size of the file. Press Return/Enter to complete the transformation.

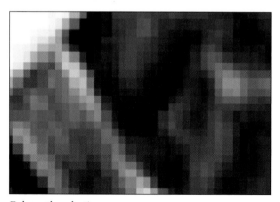

Enlarge the selection

6   Choose Filter > Blur > Gaussian Blur. Enter a small number just to soften the hard edges of the pixels. It will vary according to your file size and resolution.

This example of a 300-ppi image used a Radius of 1.2.

Choosing an Image Interpolation method

The interpolation method determines the speed and quality when resampling or transforming an image. Set the interpolation method by choosing Photoshop > Preferences > General (Mac OS X) or Edit > Preferences > General (Windows). Select one of the five options from the Image Interpolation menu. If you are working with bitmap images, choose Nearest Neighbor. This option produces jagged edges on rounded forms but will maintain sharp, straight edges for vertical and horizontal forms. Bilinear yields better speed than Bicubic, with a medium quality result. For the best detail retention, choose Bicubic (Better). Bicubic takes longer than the other choices, but the image quality is usually worth the time. Bicubic Smoother and Bicubic Sharper produce the same quality as Bicubic (Better), with the former result being slightly smoother and the latter being slightly sharper.

Original file

Nearest Neighbor (Faster)

Bilinear

Bicubic (Better)

Bicubic Smoother

Bicubic Sharper

Shortcut: Change the Liquify brush size

To change the brush size quickly while painting within the Liquify dialog box, use the [and] (the left and right bracket) keys. Press the [key to reduce the brush size by 2 pixels. Press the] key to increase the brush size by 2 pixels.

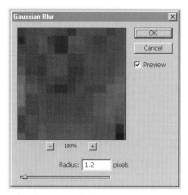

Blur the image slightly

7 Choose Filter > Liquify. In the Liquify dialog box, select the forward warp tool and set the Brush Size. Use a brush that has a diameter roughly the size of two of the color squares in your image. If you're not sure how big to make the brush, move the pointer over the image to compare the brush size to the squares.

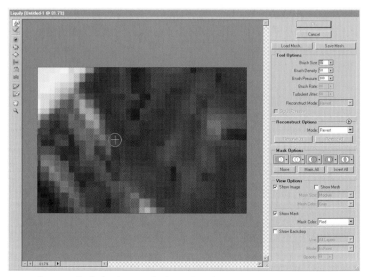

Open the Liquify dialog box and select a brush

8 Using the forward warp tool, make strokes across the image. Keep the strokes close to each other and try alternating the direction. Don't scribble back and forth; make one gentle stroke in one direction and then make another stroke right next to it in the opposite direction. If you want to swirl the colors, make the curved strokes with large, slow motions.

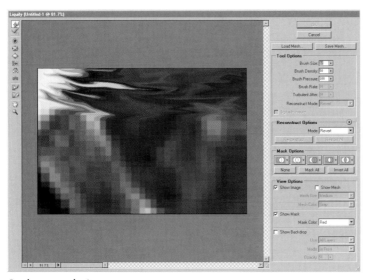

Stroke across the image

9 Once you have finished warping the image and are satisfied with the result, click OK.

Warped image

Constraining the Liquify warp strokes

To constrain the warp strokes across the image for a Bargello effect (multicolored zigzag), follow these steps.

1 In the Liquify dialog box, hold down Shift and click the image preview once with the brush.

2 Still holding down Shift, move the brush to the opposite side of the image preview and click it again.

The image is warped in a straight line. Repeat these steps above with alternating starting points for a zigzag effect.

Shift-click, Shift-click for a straight-line warp effect

Use the Hue/Saturation dialog box to create a multitude of marble papers from just one image. Just change the settings to get completely different images.

Original marble image

Hue changed to +180

Lightness changed to +25

Saturation changed to +60

10 If you want to adjust the colors or saturation of the marbled paper, choose Image > Adjustments > Hue/Saturation. Turn on the Preview option, and make your changes. If you want to place your marbled paper inside of a shape, continue with the next step.

In this example, the hue was changed to a greener color and the saturation was increased.

Adjust colors with Hue/Saturation

Colorized marbled paper

1 Duplicate Layer 1 to retain a copy of the original marble.

2 Choose Image > Adjustments > Hue/Saturation. Turn on the Preview option, and experiment with the Hue, Saturation, and Lightness values until you are satisfied with the result. Click OK.

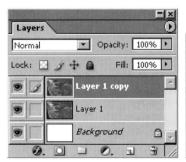

Duplicate Layer 1

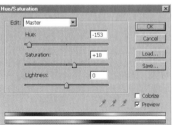

Adjust the Hue/Saturation

3   Repeat steps 1 and 2 of the Colorized Marbled Paper technique until you have as many colored marble papers as you need.

Create several marble paper layers

4   To use the marbled paper in an illustration like the following example, follow steps 8 through 14 of the Painted Paper Illustrations technique on page 42.

Don't forget to return your Image Interpolation preferences (step 4 on page 36) to Bicubic when you've finished this technique.

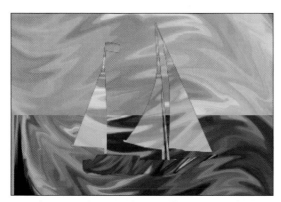

Complete using the Painted-paper Illustrations technique

Making a marbled frame

To make a marbled frame like the sample illustration on page 34, follow these steps:

1   Make a rectangular selection the size of the frame.
2   In the Channels palette, click the Save Selection as Channel button. Click the new channel thumbnail to view it.
3   With the selection still active, choose Select > Modify > Contract. Enter the amount of thickness for your frame. Click OK.
4   Fill the selection with 100% black and deselect.

5   Command/Ctrl-click the channel thumbnail to load it as a selection.
6   Select the layer that contains the marble paper image. With the selection active, click the Add Layer Mask button at the bottom of the Layers palette.
7   Add a Bevel & Emboss layer style.

5 | Painted-paper illustrations

Some illustrators use a method of collage that requires making many sheets of painted paper. The paper is then cut into shapes that are combined to form the illustration. You can create your own digitally painted collage with this technique. Create your illustration outlines in Illustrator or use Photoshop to create the paths. Then make several layers of painted paper. For each paper layer, you'll add a layer mask to mask out the collage shapes. If you want a three-dimensional look, try adding a tiny drop shadow to the shapes. This technique also works well with marbled paper (see "Marbled paper" on page 34). Just substitute the painted layer with a marbled layer.

1   Open a new RGB file in Photoshop. Create a new layer and name it Paint 1.

2   Select the brush tool in the toolbox. Choose Window > Brushes to display the Brushes palette. From the Brushes palette menu, choose Thick Heavy Brushes. In the warning dialog box, click Append to add the brushes to the existing list.

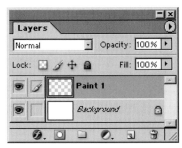

Create the paint layer

Click Append to add brushes

3   Scroll to the bottom of the list in the Brushes palette, and select the Flat Bristle brush. Depending on your file size, you may want to adjust the size of the brush. If so, increase or decrease the Master Diameter of the brush now.

4   Choose a foreground color, and in the tool options bar, set the tool mode to Hard Light.

Naming layers

It's a good idea to name your layers so that you can keep track of them more easily. You can name or rename layers several ways.

- When creating a new layer, Option/Alt-click the New Layer button at the bottom of the Layers palette to create a new layer and name it at the same time.
- Double-click the layer name in the Layers palette to select the name; then type a new name. Press Return/Enter to apply the name.
- Option/Alt–double-click the layer name in the Layers palette to display the Layer Properties dialog box. Enter a new name and click OK.
- Select a layer in the Layers palette and choose Layer Properties from the palette menu. Enter a new name and click OK.

Shortcut: Change blending modes

For a quick way to cycle through the blending modes while you paint, hold down the Shift key and press the + [plus] or − [minus] key.

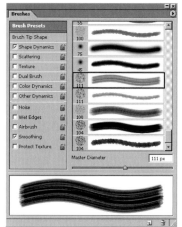

Select the Flat Bristle brush

Choose Hard Light mode

5 Begin to paint the entire layer with the textured brush. Overlap the brush strokes for additional color and texture changes. Use the brush at different sizes and modes.

Set the brush to Multiply, Difference, or Vivid Light for different effects.

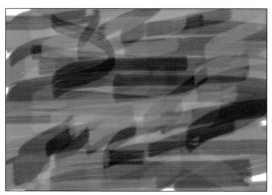

Paint the first layer with the textured brush

6 Create a new layer and name it Paint 2. Hide the Paint 1 layer.

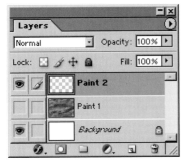

Hide the Paint 1 layer and create the Paint 2 layer

7 Repeat steps 3 through 6 for as many colors as you need for your illustration. Try using some of the other brushes for different textures. Try painting two or three similiar colors on the same layer.

Paint subsequent layers with textured brushes

8 If you are not copying the illustration paths from Illustrator, make an illustration with paths in Photoshop, and skip to step 11. If you are copying paths from Illustrator, open the illustration file in Illustrator. Choose Illustrator > Preferences > File Handling & Clipboard (Mac OS X) or Edit > Preferences > File Handling & Clipboard (Windows). Select the AICB option, and choose Preserve Paths. Click OK.

Varying the brush size

To change brush sizes quickly as you paint, press the [and] (left and right bracket) keys. Press the [key to reduce the size and the] key to increase the brush size. The increment of change depends on the brush size. A brush size between 0 to 100 pixels will change by 10-pixel increments. A brush between 100 to 200 pixels will change by 25-pixel increments. A brush between 200 to 300 will change by 50 pixels. A brush size between 300 to 2500 pixels will change by 100 pixels each time you use this shortcut.

Transforming paths

If you want to adjust the size of paths before you make them into masks, select the paths with the path selection tool. Then choose Edit > Free Transform Path to scale the path. Press Return/Enter to complete the transformation.

9 In Illustrator, select the illustration paths, and choose Edit > Copy.

10 Switch back to Photoshop, and choose Edit > Paste. In the dialog box that appears, select Path and click OK.

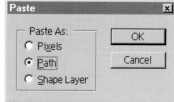

Copy paths   *Choose Paste As Path*

11 In the Paths palette, click the Work Path if it's not already selected. Choose the path selection tool and click one of the paths. Click the Load Path as Selection button at the bottom of the Paths palette.

Paint subsequent layers with textured brushes

12 Click in the blank area of the Paths palette to hide the paths from view. In the Layers palette, click the layer that you'll fill with the selection. Make sure that the layer is not hidden, and click the Add Layer Mask button.

13 If you want to rotate or scale the texture, unlink the mask from its layer. Click the layer thumbnail, and move, scale, or rotate the layer image. Using the Edit > Free Transform command, make the transformations needed, and press Return/Enter.

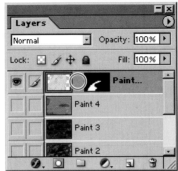

Add a layer mask

Unlink the mask from the layer

14 Repeat steps 11 through 13 for each of the paint layers that you made. Remember, you can select multiple objects and put them on one layer mask. In this example, the faces and hands are all on one layer mask.

Completed illustration

6 | Stippling

Different colors spatter-painted or airbrushed on top of each other creates a rich textural look. Using several different colors for shadows instead of just black creates a richer effect. As an alternative, you can add dimension and character to your type or graphics using textured gradations. First, build a different layer for each color you want to spatter onto your image. Then add a layer mask and texturize it. You'll end up with a very versatile multilayered file. You can experiment with different colors, layer modes, and textures as you lay one colored texture on top of another.

Basic stippling

1   Create a basic design with flat shapes of color. Make a separate layer for each different colored object.

If you use graphics created in Illustrator, export them in the Photoshop (PSD) format. Choose the Write Layers option and open the file in Photoshop. Set the resolution depending on how coarse or fine you want the stipple texture: The higher the resolution is, the finer the stipple texture.

Create a basic design

2   Select the layer of the first graphic you want to texturize. Make a copy of that layer by Option/Alt-dragging it onto the New Layer button at the bottom of the Layers palette.

Shortcut: Fill while keeping transparency

To fill a layer as though Lock Transparent Pixels were turned on, use these keystrokes:
- Mac OS X: press Option+Shift+Delete to fill with the foreground color. Press Command+Shift+Delete to fill with the background color.
- Windows: press Alt+Shift+ Backspace to fill with the foreground color. Press Ctrl+Shift+Backspace to fill with the background color.

Name the new layer Texture 1. Select the Lock Transparent pixels option.

If the layer is a type layer, the transparent pixels are locked automatically.

3 Choose a color that you want to stipple onto the base color of the original shape.

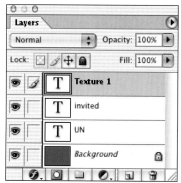 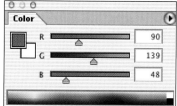

Create the Texture 1 layer   *Select a stipple color*

4 Fill the Texture 1 layer with the foreground color. A shortcut for filling with the foreground color is Option+Delete (Mac OS X) or Alt+Backspace (Windows).

Don't worry about the color covering up the original. The stipple texture will be applied in the next few steps.

Fill Texture 1 layer with the foreground color

5   Option/Alt-click the Add Layer Mask button at the bottom of the Layers palette to add a layer mask to the Texture 1 layer.

Pressing the Option/Alt key fills the layer mask with black, which blocks out the new color until you change it.

6   With the layer mask still selected, choose Filter > Noise > Add Noise. Turn on the Preview option so that you can see the effect on your image. When you have the amount of color and texture that looks good with your graphic, click OK.

To see what noise looks like at different resolutions, see "Choosing the right amounts for noise and grain" on page 293.

Shortcut: View the layer mask channel

To view a layer mask without seeing its layer image, Option/Alt-click the layer mask thumbnail in the Layers palette. To return to the layer view, Option/Alt-click the layer mask thumbnail again.

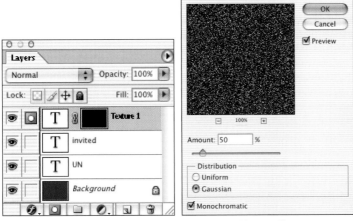

Create a black layer mask   Apply the Add Noise filter

7   Evaluate the result. If you don't want to add any more stipple colors to this graphic, repeat steps 2 through 7 for any other layers in your file that need stippling. For multicolor stippling, continue with step 8.

You may be satisfied with adding just one color, but mixing at least two or three colors together produces a richer effect.

Shortcut: Change the paint opacity from the keyboard

To change the paint opacity quickly while painting, use the number keys. Press the 1 key to change the opacity to 10%. Press the 2 key to change the opacity to 20% and so on. The 0 key returns the opacity to 100%.

Evaluate the results

8 Repeat steps 2 through 5 and name the new layer Texture 2.

9 Reapply the Add Noise filter just as you did in step 6, but this time use a different amount. In this example, the Noise amount was increased to get more purple dots than green.

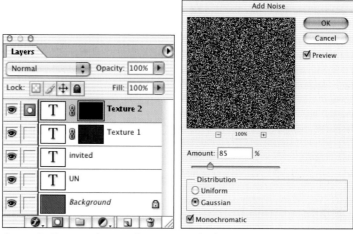

Create the Texture 2 layer with a mask

Apply the Add Noise filter

10 Repeat steps 8 and 9 for as many colors as you want to add. Stop and save the file, or continue with the next step if you want to create a stippled gradation.

Multiple stipple colors applied

Shortcut: Turn a layer mask on and off

To turn a layer mask on or off, Shift-click the layer mask thumbnail in the Layers palette. The layer mask will still be there, but a large red X will indicate that it is hidden. To turn the layer mask back on, Shift-click the layer mask thumbnail again.

Stippled gradients

1 Make a new layer and position it directly over the layer you want to stipple. Name the layer Gradient Texture 1.

This example will show a textured gradient added to the background. If you want the textured gradient applied to a shape on a layer, Option/Alt-click the line between the layers in the Layers palette to create a clipping mask.

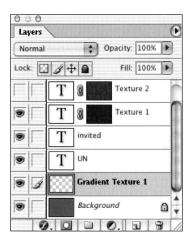

Create the Gradient Texture layer

2 Change the foreground color to the color you want to use for the stippled gradation. Select the gradient tool in the toolbox. In the tool options bar, click the Linear Gradient

Applying gradients precisely

To control the angle of a gradient, press Shift to constrain the angle to 45° or 90°. If you want the entire gradient to show, drag from edge to edge of the selection. If you want only part to show, drag from outside the selection.

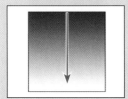

Shift-drag from top to bottom for a full gradient.

Shift-drag from corner to corner for an angled gradient.

Shift-drag from edge to middle for a short gradient.

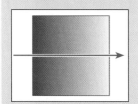

Shift-drag from outside to outside for a partial gradient.

button and click the arrow button next to the gradient sample to display the Gradient pop-up palette. Change the Gradient type to Foreground to Transparent.

3 Apply a gradient to the Gradient Texture 1 layer with the gradient tool.

Don't worry if you have applied too much color at this point. You can control the amount of color added by how much noise you use in the next step.

Create a gradient on the Gradient Texture 1 layer

4 Option/Alt-click the Add Layer Mask button at the bottom of the Layers palette to add a layer mask to the Gradient Texture 1 layer.

5 With the layer mask still selected, choose Filter > Noise > Add Noise. Turn on the Preview option so that you can see the effect on your image. When you have the amount of color and texture that looks good with your graphic, click OK.

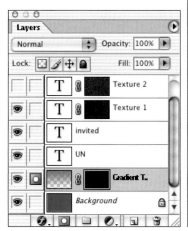

Add a black layer mask

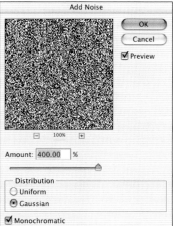

Apply the Add Noise filter

6 Evaluate the result. If you don't want to add any more stipple colors to this gradient, repeat steps 1 through 5 of this technique for any other gradients that need stippling. For multicolor stippling, continue with step 7.

Remember, stippling with at least two or three different colors together produces a richer effect.

Evaluate the result

7 Repeat steps 1 through 4 using a different foreground color and name the new layer Gradient Texture 2.

Stippling to change colors or values

You can use stippling not only to add texture to your graphics but also to vary the colors. For example, you can warm a red by adding a touch of yellow. You can also lighten or darken a color by using a tint or tone of the same hue. The following examples show the base color on the left and the colors added in sequence on the right.

Red   *+ Gold*   *+ Green*

Blue   *+ Red*   *+ Gold*

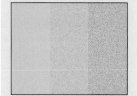

Gold   *+ Orange + Red*

Blue   *+ Purple + Magenta*

Painting with a stipple texture

To use the stipple texture when you paint with a brush, set the brush's mode to Dissolve and lower the brush's opacity. The lower the opacity, the more space between the pixels or stippling. The higher the opacity, the denser the brushstroke will be.

Set the brush mode to Dissolve and lower the opacity

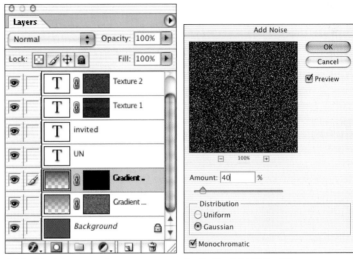

Add a black layer mask   *Apply the Add Noise filter*

8 Reapply the Add Noise filter just as you did in step 5, but this time use a different amount. In this example, the Noise amount was decreased to get fewer teal dots than green.

9 Add the stipple texture to the remaining elements in your design.

Shadows have color and texture, too, so don't forget to stipple the shaded areas with several colors instead of leaving them black. This example shows a 60% gray-blue drop shadow added and its blending mode set to Multiply.

Brushstroke resembles stippling texture

Variation: Coarser stippling

To make the stippling a bit larger and more irregular in texture, try this variation. Note that the colors will look different because the stipple texture is coarser.

1   Follow the Basic Stippling or Stippled Gradients technique.

2   In the Layers palette, click one of the stippled layer masks to select it.

3   Choose Filter > Noise > Median. Turn on the Preview option and experiment with the Radius value until you like the effect. Click OK.

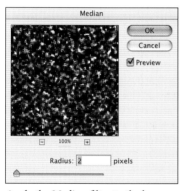

Apply the Median filter to the layer mask

4   Repeat steps 2 and 3 for each layer mask.

This example uses the Median filter with a value of 2 pixels.

Applying filters to the layer mask

You can add more texture or change the stippling by applying a filter to the layer mask. See the Variation for instructions. Here are some other filters to try.

Original layer mask made with Noise of 50% (300 ppi)

Filter > Brush Strokes > Spatter: Spray Radius = 10, Smoothness = 5

Filter > Texture > Grain: Intensity = 37, Contrast = 69, Type = Clumped

Filter > Texture > Grain: Intensity = 57, Contrast = 21, Type = Enlarged

7 | Painted foliage

The Photoshop Brushes palette offers so many options, it is the perfect tool for creating brushes that can paint leaves, grass, flowers, and fields of grain. You can make an endless number of brushes to paint foliage. In this technique you'll create a leaf shape and define it as a brush. Then you'll customize it so that painting with the brush produces a stream of randomly placed, rotated, scaled, and colored leaves—just as in nature. Try using several brushes on one tree or bush. If you want striped leaves, add a subtle, dark-gray stripe to the black leaf before you define it as a brush.

1   Open a new file. Press the D key to return the foreground and background colors to the defaults. Select the pen tool in the toolbox. Select the Shape Layers option in the tool options bar.

2   Draw a leaf shape with the pen tool. (This technique shows drawing a leaf, but you can use these instructions for grass or flowers as well.)

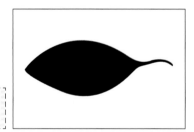

Select the Shape Layers option   *Draw a shape*

3   Choose Layer > Rasterize > Shape to change the vector shape into a raster shape. Double-click the Shape layer name, and change its name to Leaf Shape.

It's necessary to rasterize the shape because brushes can only be created from raster shapes or images. You will define the brush in the next step.

Varying a brush's opacity

You can make a brush out of any image selected with a rectangular marquee. If you use a color or grayscale image instead of a 100% black image, the brush's opacity will vary. The areas of the brush tip shape that are 100% black will be opaque. The areas of the brush tip shape that are less than 100% will be transparent. The lighter the gray, the more transparent that area of the brush will be.

Brush tip shape is 100% black

Brush tip shape is 50% black

Viewing brushes in the Brushes palette

Set the viewing preference for your Brushes palette so that you can find your brushes more easily. To see both the brush thumbnail and its name, choose Small List or Large List from the Brushes palette menu. To view just the name, choose Text Only. If you like viewing a thumbnail of the brushstrokes, choose Stroke Thumbnail. Sometimes the thumbnails of brushes and their strokes can look very similar, so be sure to name each brush carefully as you create them. Careful naming will make it much easier for you to select different brushes as you paint.

4   With the Leaf Shape layer still selected in the Layers palette, choose Edit > Define Brush Preset. Name the brush Leaf 1, and click OK in the Brush Name dialog box.

Rasterize the shape   *Define a new brush*

5   Select the brush tool in the toolbox. Choose Window > Brushes to display the Brushes palette. Click Brush Tip Shape on the left side of the palette, scroll through the list, and click the Leaf 1 brush. If desired, adjust the diameter.

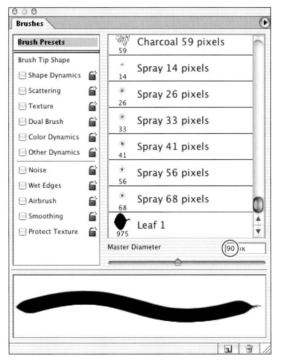

Select the leaf brush and change its diameter

6 Click the name Shape Dynamics in the list on the left side of the Brushes palette. Clicking the words automatically selects the option and displays its controls. Adjust the Size Jitter and the Angle Jitter using the preview at the bottom of the palette.

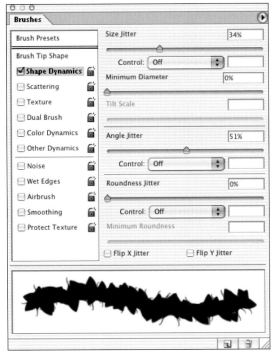

Adjust the Shape Dynamics

7 Click the name Scattering in the list on the left side of the Brushes palette. Adjust the Scatter, Count, and Count Jitter (randomness).

Controlling the direction of grass

Some foliage grows in a haphazard way with leaves turned in all directions. Some leaves and flowers grow in one direction due to wind or gravity. To depict direction, whether uniform or haphazard, change the shape dynamics of your foliage brush. Adjust the Angle Jitter to control the amount of leaf rotation. A larger percentage will result in more rotation of the leaves. A small percentage will ensure that the leaves are placed at a similar angle to each other.

For example, the grass images below have just a 4% Angle Jitter. This gives them a slightly different angle from each other. Also, the bottom example uses the Flip X Jitter option to make the grass look a bit more random. The top example doesn't use this option and thus looks more like wind-blown dune grass.

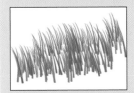

Flip X Jitter turned off

Flip X Jitter turned on

Controlling the Hue Jitter

To change the foliage color as you paint, select the Color Dynamics option for your brush. You can change colors by specifying a Hue Jitter percentage. First, select a foreground color from the Color palette. Then enter a value for the Hue Jitter percentage in the Color Dynamics section of the Brushes palette. The larger the percentage, the more the hue will change as you paint.

If you want to better visualize how Hue Jitter works, change the Color palette display to HSB Sliders using the palette menu. Then slide the H slider back and forth to see the Hue change.

10% Hue Jitter

25% Hue Jitter

50% Hue Jitter

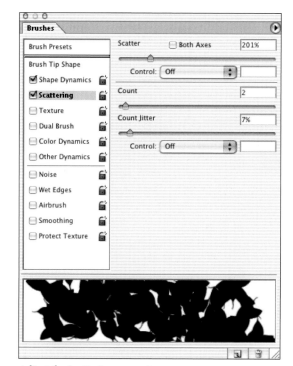

Adjust the Scattering amount

8 Click the name Color Dynamics in the list on the left side of the Brushes palette. Adjust the Hue Jitter.

You won't be able to preview the hue change until you actually paint—so guess. Hue Jitter specifies how much the foreground color will vary in hue with each brush stroke.

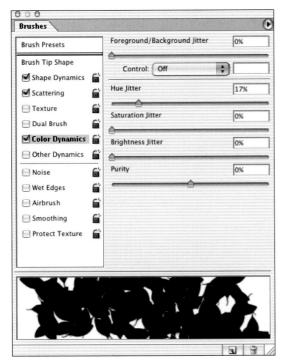

Adjust the Color Dynamics

9 Click the New Brush button at the bottom of the Brushes palette. Name this brush Leaf 2.

Because you changed the dynamics and options of the Leaf 1 brush, you must save it as a new brush. Each time you change an option on a custom brush, you must resave the brush or the changes will be lost.

10 Create a new layer, and name it Brush Test. Turn off the Leaf Shape layer.

Controlling Hue Jitter color changes

A good way to control the color changes as you paint is to choose the two colors that will define the range of color change. First, select a foreground and background color. The foreground color will be the main color. The background color will mix into the foreground color according to the percentage you specify. Select a percentage for the Foreground/Background Jitter. The higher the percentage, the more background color will be mixed into the foreground color as you paint.

Set foreground and background colors

50% Foreground/Background Jitter

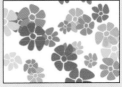

100% Foreground/Background Jitter

Painting foliage behind foliage

Want to paint some foilage behind some that you've already painted? As long as you painted the first foliage on a new, transparent layer, you can paint behind it by selecting the Behind mode from the Modes menu in the tool options bar. Painting more foliage on the transparent layer will paint behind what is already there without covering it up.

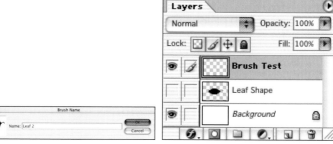

Save the new brush

Create a test layer

Paint the frontmost foliage

Painting other foliage behind the frontmost foliage

11 Select a foreground color that will be the basic leaf hue.

12 Use the brush tool to paint a few strokes on the Brush Test layer to test your brush. Evaluate the color, size, scatter amount, and number of leaves; then decide what you want to change.

You may want to change the brush settings in the tool options bar, too. For example, setting the blending mode to Color or Multiply produces a transparent, overlapping effect.

Test the brush

13 Notice the effect of changing several options on the brush in this example. The Scatter amount, Size Jitter, and Hue Jitter were increased; the Angle Jitter was decreased, and a Brightness Jitter was added.

Adjust the settings and test the brush again

14 Once you've created several brushes that you want to use again, save them as a brush library. Choose Save Brushes from the Brushes palette menu. Save them in the Presets/ Brushes folder, inside the Photoshop application folder; the library name will appear alphabetically in the Brushes palette menu after you restart Photoshop.

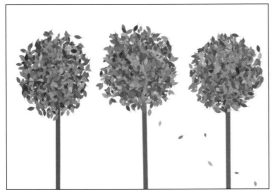

Completed illustration

Using paths to paint defined shapes

To paint foliage along a specific line or around a shape, use paths. Follow these steps:

1 Select the brush tool in the toolbox. Then select a foliage brush in the Brushes palette.
2 Draw the path along which you will apply the foliage.
3 Save the path by double-clicking it in the Paths palette.
4 Choose Stroke Path from the Paths palette menu. In the Stroke Path dialog box, choose Brush from the pop-up menu. Click OK.

You may have to change the size of the brush depending on the size of the path; simply select Edit > Undo and change the brush diameter. Then repeat the steps again beginning with step 4.

Create a path

Stroke the path with a foliage brush

8 | Seamless patterns

Aesculus Californica

CALIFORNIA BUCKEYE

You can make a pattern in Photoshop in a couple of ways. Use the Pattern Maker to make many patterns based on a selection of pixels; Pattern Maker is quick and easy to use but doesn't give you control of the pattern tile. (See the Photoshop CS user guide or Photoshop Help for more on this feature.) Or simply select an area using the rectangle marquee tool and then choose Edit > Define Pattern. Almost always, however, filling an area with this type of pattern leaves telltale tiling seams, or grids. The following technique shows how to create a pattern tile with edges that won't be visible when the tile repeats. The types of images that work best with this technique have soft, blurry backgrounds or plenty of texture. Images with strong lines don't work well because it's hard to match up the lines at the proper angle.

1   Open the image that contains the area you want to use for a pattern tile.

Images with plain or textured backgrounds make the best seamless patterns because their tile lines are easier to smooth away. Images that bleed off the edge of the tile and images with gradations are less desirable because they are more difficult to touch up.

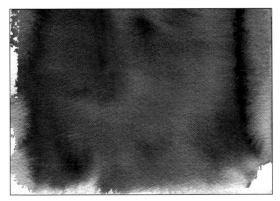

Open an image

What are good images for textured backgrounds?

- Rocks
- Papers
- Fields of grass or grain
- Clouds
- Wood grain
- Marble
- Plaster
- Fabric
- Tree bark
- Small plants and flowers
- Rusted metal
- Concrete

Shortcut: Expand the canvas

You can add to the canvas size with the crop tool without resampling the image. Here's how:

1 Zoom out on your image so that you can see the gray area around the image. You may need to enlarge the window size to see the gray area.
2 Start in the gray area and, using the crop tool, draw a rectangle. Because you are drawing outside the image area, a selection will appear around the image edge.
3 Now adjust the handles to enlarge the cropping area. To enlarge it from the center of the image, hold down Option/Alt as you drag a corner handle.
4 Press Return/Enter to complete the crop. The canvas size will now be increased by whatever amount you dragged beyond the image edge.

2 Select the crop tool in the toolbox, and crop the image to the size and area you want the pattern tile to be.

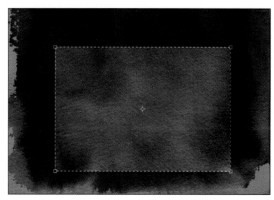

Use the crop tool to select the pattern tile area

3 Choose File > Save As and give the pattern tile file a new name.

Naming the pattern tile file ensures that the original file stays intact. You may want to use it again later.

4 Choose Filter > Other > Offset. Select the Wrap Around option; for the horizontal and vertical values, drag the sliders to approximately half the value of the width and height. Turn on the Preview option to make sure that the image is chopped into four approximately equal pieces.

This filter slices up your image and moves it horizontally and vertically. It is helpful to offset the image so that you can see how the edges of the pattern tiles will meet. Click OK.

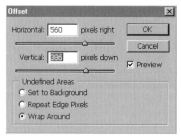

Use the Offset filter

5 Examine the result.

The Offset filter splits the image into four sections. Notice that the left half of the image completes the right half, and the top half of the image completes the bottom half. The seams you see would be visible had you taken the cropped image from step 2 and used it as a pattern tile.

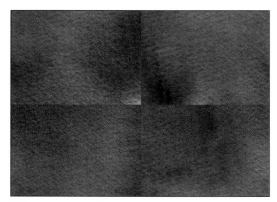

Offset the pattern tile

6 Select the healing brush tool in the toolbox. Choose the Sampled option in the options bar. The Sampled option lets you sample texture from other parts of the image and paint with it to cover up the seams.

Note: If your pattern contains clearly defined objects such as stones, beads, leaves or flowers, in the options bar try changing the mode to Replace instead of Normal and choose the Aligned option. The Aligned option works just like the clone stamp tool.

7 Select a brush that is similar in size and softness to the object or texture you will clone. Option/Alt-click to sample an image or texture area that you want to clone over the seam.

In this example, a small, soft-edged brush was used because the texture is slightly soft and fine-grained.

Normal versus Replace modes with the healing brush

When set to Normal mode, the healing brush samples the texture, color, and brightness of the target area and then melds what you paint. Normal mode works well for very textured subject matter like the watercolor paper at left. In the following examples, compare the two brush modes. Try using Replace mode when painting in hard-edged shapes like the berries shown here.

Option/Alt-click to sample

Paint with Replace mode

Paint with Normal mode

Shortcut: Change brush sizes from the keyboard

To change the brush size quickly while painting, use the [and] (left and right bracket) keys. Press the [key to reduce the brush size by 2 pixels. Press the] key to increase the brush size by 2 pixels.

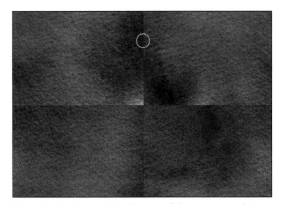

Use a brush that matches the size of the texture or objects

8   Eliminate the center seams between the four sections of the image by sampling a texture and then painting it on top of the seam. Try to paint using many short brush strokes so that the stroke itself is not visible. Sometimes just one mouse-click instead of dragging is more effective.

The goal is to try to blend the backgrounds of each rectangle together.

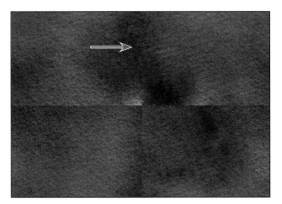

Begin to paint over the seam

9   Continue sampling and cloning until you have covered the seams.

Be prepared to spend some time on this step. Depending on the image, it can take quite a while to cover up the seams.

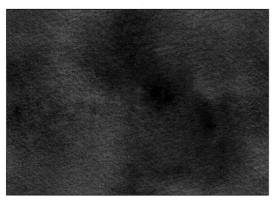

Cover all the seams

10 Choose Filter > Other > Offset to check your work. The values that you used in step 4 should reverse the offset effect. Click OK.

11 Choose Select > All; then choose Edit > Define Pattern.

12 Create a new file to test the pattern fill. Make sure that the file is several times larger than the pattern tile. Select a large area (or the entire file) and choose Edit > Fill. From the Use menu, choose Pattern. Select the pattern tile and click OK.

13 Evaluate the overall look of the pattern and identify any problem areas. If you like the effect, save the pattern tile file. If you want to touch up the tile, repeat steps 4 through 13.

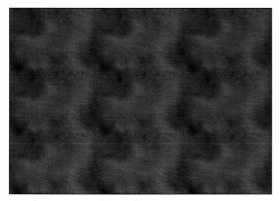

Test the pattern in a larger file

Saving patterns in a library

If you want to use your patterns again in other files, save the pattern tiles you've created as a library.

1 Open a Pattern palette by clicking the Pattern pop-up palette in the options bar. The Pattern pop-up palette appears in the options bar for the healing brush, paint bucket, and pattern stamp tools. The Pattern pop-up palette also appears in the Fill dialog box when you choose Pattern from the Use menu.

2 From the Pattern pop-up palette menu, choose Save Patterns. Name the library and click OK. The new library is placed in the Patterns folder, and the new pattern library name will appear in the list of pattern libraries available in the Pattern pop-up palette menu.

9 Stone and stucco textures

With Photoshop, it's possible to compress geologic eons into virtual moments. Here are techniques for creating stone and synthetic textures—including sandstone, marble, and stucco—in minutes using Photoshop filters. Tips also show you how to create granite and brick textures, and recolor textures for other projects. These textures make great surfaces and backgrounds. The process of creating them is similar to that of the wood-grain textures, described in the "Wood-grain textures" on page 84. Each time you make the stone and stucco textures, results will vary because the filters never give the exact same result twice. So it's important to save the textures for reuse later. It's also a good idea to make the texture files larger than needed so that you can copy and paste different parts of them at different times.

Sandstone

1   Create a new file. Return the foreground and background colors to their defaults by pressing the D key.

2   Choose Filter > Render > Difference Clouds.

Note: If you use this filter on a new layer instead of the Background layer, first fill the layer with white. The filter won't work on a transparent layer.

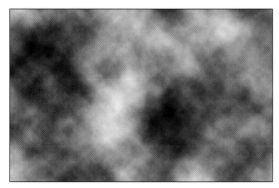

Apply the Difference Clouds filter

Creating different sandstone colors

The Sandstone technique shows you how to create a warm, yellow stone surface. Follow the technique and then change the gradient map colors in step 5 to these values to get the colors shown in the following examples.

Left stop: R = 237, G = 235, B = 213
Middle stop: R = 211, G = 201, B = 146
Right stop: R = 0, G = 0, B = 0

Left stop: R = 255, G = 255, B = 255
Middle stop: R = 177, G = 106, B = 36
Right stop: R = 0, G = 0, B = 0

Left stop: R = 255, G = 255, B = 255
Middle stop: R = 147, G = 152, B = 176
Right stop: R = 0, G = 0, B = 0

3   Press Command/Ctrl+F to reapply the Difference Clouds filter. Repeat this step until you have applied the filter a total of five times, including the time in step 2.

Unlike the other Render filters, Difference Clouds has a cumulative effect. Each time you apply it, the existing image is altered instead of replaced.

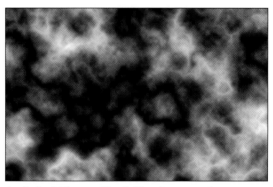

Apply the Difference Clouds filter four more times

4   Choose Filter > Stylize > Emboss. Start with the values shown in the following illustration and then adjust to your preference.

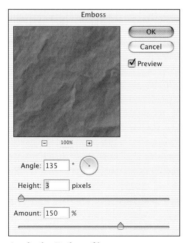

Apply the Emboss filter

5   Select the gradient tool in the toolbox. Click the gradient
    swatch in the tool options bar to open the Gradient Editor.
    Create a gradient that will contain the light, medium, and
    dark values in the sandstone. If you want to match the color
    in the example in step 6, enter these values:

    - Left gradient stop: R = 255, G = 251, B = 204;

    - Middle gradient stop: R = 211, G = 190, B = 71; and

    - Right gradient stop: R = 26, G = 11, B = 35.

Name the gradient Sandstone and click the New button. Click
OK to exit the Gradient Editor.

6   Click the New Adjustment Layer button at the bottom of
    the Layers palette and choose Gradient Map from the pop-
    up menu. In the Gradient Map dialog box, click the triangle
    to the right of the gradient swatch and select the Sandstone
    gradient. Turn on the Preview option. If you don't like the
    colors, click the gradient swatch and adjust them until you
    like the preview. When you are satisfied, click OK.

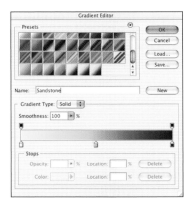

Create a Sandstone gradient   *Add a Gradient Map adjustment layer*

7   Evaluate the effect. If you want to use the sandstone texture
    in another file, you must combine all the layers onto one
    layer. To keep the original layers intact, create a new layer
    and name it Merged Sandstone. Move it to the top of the
    list in the Layers palette. With the Merged Sandstone layer

selected, press Option/Alt and choose Merge Visible from the Layers palette menu. The sandstone texture can now be copied or transformed as desired. If you are satisfied with the effect, save the file. To add a bit more texture, continue with step 8.

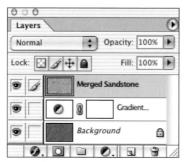

Create the Merged Sandstone layer

8   To add just a bit more sand texture to the sandstone, choose Filter > Texture > Texturizer. Use the following settings: Texture = Sandstone, Scaling = 100, Relief = 2, and Light = Top left. Click OK.

Apply the Texturizer filter to add grainy texture

Stucco

1   Create a new file larger than the size of the stucco surface you will use. (This allows room for cropping out areas you may not want to use later.)

2   Press the D key to return the foreground and background colors to their defaults. Choose Filter > Sketch > Note Paper. Use these settings: Image Balance = 1, Graininess = 8, and Relief = 11. Click OK.

Note: If you use this filter on a new layer instead of the Background layer, first fill the layer with white. The filter won't work on a transparent layer.

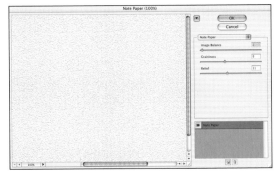

Apply the Note Paper filter

3   If you want an even, fine-textured stucco, skip to step 5. If you want to introduce a few spots and flaws to make the stucco look a bit more realistic, Option/Alt-click the New Layer button at the bottom of the Layers palette. Choose the Color Dodge mode and select the Fill with Color-Dodge-Neutral Color (Black) option. Name the layer Spots and click OK.

Filling the layer with color lets you use the filter in the next step. Some filters work only if the layer contains pixels. Some can work on transparent, or empty, layers.

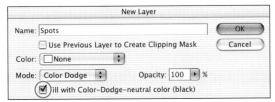

Create a new layer set to Color Dodge mode and filled with Color-Dodge-Neutral Color (Black)

Filling layers with a mode-neutral color

Some filters won't work on a transparent layer. To apply a texture to a layer and set its blending mode to affect the layers beneath it, you may have to fill the layer with a mode-neutral color. A mode-neutral color is a color that is not affected by the layer's blending mode. For example, on a layer with a blending mode of Multiply, the white pixels are not affected, so white is the mode-neutral color for Multiply.

You can create a layer, set its layer mode, and fill it with a mode-neutral color, all in one step. Here's how:

1   Option/Alt-click the New Layer button at the bottom of the Layers palette.

2   In the New Layer dialog box, select the blending mode. If the selected mode has a neutral color fill available, select the Fill with Neutral Color option and click OK.

The image appearance won't change until you add something to the new layer.

Select the Fill with Neutral Color option

The blending modes that do not have a mode-neutral color option are Normal, Dissolve, Hard Mix, Hue, Saturation, Color, and Luminosity.

Creating a brick wall

Your stucco wall can turn into a brick wall in a matter of moments.

1 Press the D key to reset the default foreground and background colors.
2 Option/Alt-click the New Layer button at the bottom of the Layers palette. Choose Linear Burn mode and select the Fill with Linear Burn-Neutral Color option. Click OK.
3 Choose Filter > Texture > Texturizer. Select Brick as the texture and adjust the settings for your image. Click OK.
4 If the brick image is too light, choose Image > Adjustments > Levels. Drag the black slider to the right to darken the brick outlines. When you are satisfied with the result, click OK.

4 With the Spots layer selected, choose Filter > Artistic > Sponge. Use the following values: Brush Size = 0, Definition = 25, and Smoothness = 15. Click OK.

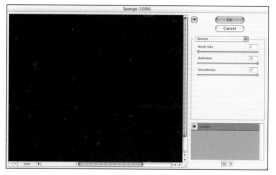

Apply the Sponge filter to the Spots layer

5 To colorize the stucco, Option/Alt-click the New Adjustment layer button at the bottom of the Layers palette. Select Solid Color from the pop-up menu. Choose Linear Burn as the mode and click OK. When the color picker appears, select the color for your stucco. The color mix used in the example is R = 211, G = 195, and B = 171. Click OK.

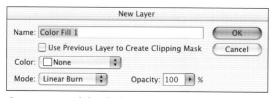

Create a new Solid Color layer set to Linear Burn mode

6 Evaluate the effect. If you want to use the stucco texture in another file, you must combine all the layers onto one layer. To keep the original layers intact, create a new layer and name it Merged Stucco. Move it to the top of the list in the Layers palette. With the Merged Stucco layer selected, press Option/Alt and choose Merge Visible from the Layers palette menu. The stucco texture can now be copied or transformed as desired.

Completed stucco texture

Marble

1   Create a new file. Return the foreground and background colors to their defaults by pressing the D key.

2   Choose Filter > Render > Difference Clouds.

Apply the Difference Clouds filter

3   Press Command/Ctrl+F to reapply the Difference Clouds filter. Repeat this step until you have the amount of marbling you desire. This example used the filter four times.

The Difference Clouds has a cumulative effect. Each time you apply it, the existing image is altered instead of replaced.

Creating granite

Whip up some granite in just a few quick steps.

1   Press the D key to reset the default foreground and background colors.

2   Create a new layer and fill it with white by pressing Command/Ctrl+Delete/ Backspace.

3   Choose Filter > Render > Fibers. Use these settings: Variance = 64, Strength = 3.

4   Choose Filter > Texture > Craquelure. Use these settings: Crack Spacing = 2, Crack Depth = 0, and Crack Brightness = 5.

5   Change colors by clicking the New Adjustment Layer button at the bottom of the Layers palette. Select Color Balance from the pop-up menu. Change colors and click OK.

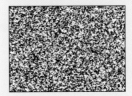

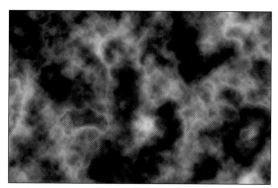

Apply the Difference Clouds filter until well marbled

4   To soften the dramatic contrast a little, click the New Adjustment Layer button at the bottom of the Layers palette. Choose Brightness/Contrast and lower the contrast to about −40. Click OK.

The good thing about adjustment layers is that you can go back and change them at any time. If you want to adjust the amount of contrast after you've applied color to the marble, just double-click the adjustment layer thumbnail and change the settings.

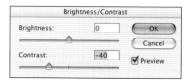

Add a Brightness/Contrast adjustment layer

5   To add color to the marble, create another layer by Option/ Alt-clicking the New Layer button at the bottom of the Layers palette. Name the new layer Colors, set its mode to Hard Light, and click OK.

6   Using the Color palette, change the foreground and background colors to two similar colors you would like in the marble. In this example two greens were selected. The dark green mix is R = 56, G = 98, B = 79. The lighter green mix is R = 103, G = 144, and B = 111.

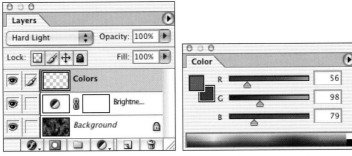

Create the Colors layer

Choose new foreground and
background colors

7   Choose Filter > Render > Clouds. Evaluate the effect. If
you want to reuse the Clouds filter to get a slightly different
effect, reapply it by pressing Command/Ctrl+F.

The Clouds filter, unlike Difference Clouds, is not cumulative. It
will replace the image each time you use it. If you don't like the
colors, change the foreground or background colors and then
reapply the Clouds filter until you are satisfied with the effect.

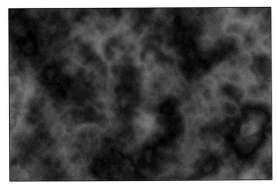

Apply the Clouds filter to the Colors layer

8   Before applying needed sharpening to the marble, combine
all layers onto one layer. Create a new layer by Option/Alt-
clicking the New Layer button at the bottom of the Layers
palette. Name the new layer Merged Marble and click OK.

9   To merge all the layers onto the Merged Marble layer, press Option/Alt and choose Merge Visible from the Layers palette menu.

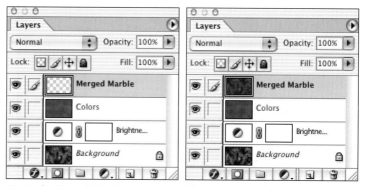

Create the Merged Marble layer   *Choose Option/Alt+Merge Visible*

10 To sharpen the veins in the marble, choose Filter > Sharpen > Unsharp Mask. Start with the settings shown here and then adjust for your image. Increasing the Radius will increase the contrast and the amount of veins in the marble. Don't increase the Threshold, because it will blur the marble more. When you are satisfied with the effect, click OK.

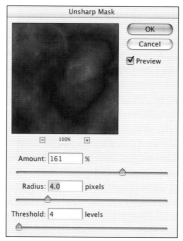

Apply the Unsharp Mask filter to the Merged Marble layer

11 Evaluate the result. If you are satisfied, save the file. If you want to change the color, continue with step 12.

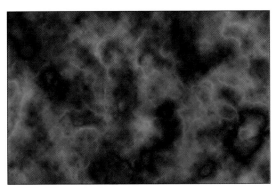

Finished Merged Marble image

12 To change the color of the marble, either go back to step 6 and, using new colors, repeat steps 6 through 11; or simply create an adjustment layer to change the colors on the Merged Marble layer. To create an adjustment layer, select the Merged Marble layer and then click the New Adjustment layer button at the bottom of the Layers palette. (Selecting the layer ensures that the adjustment layer will be placed directly above it.) Choose Color Balance from the pop-up menu. Change the values for the Shadows, Midtones, and Highlights and click OK. Save the file.

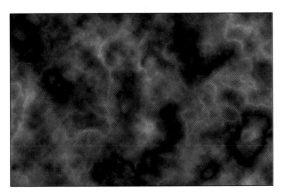

Colorized Merged Marble image

Creating different marble colors

The Marble technique shows you how to create a rich, green marble surface. Follow the technique and then in step 6, change the foreground and background colors to the following values to get the colors shown in the examples.

Foreground: R = 173, G = 155, B = 171
Background: R = 182, G = 165, B = 191

Foreground: R = 168, G = 162, B = 150
Background: R = 206, G = 200, B = 193

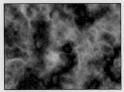

Foreground: R = 103, G = 128, B = 133
Background: R = 85, G = 137, B = 139

10 | Wood-grain textures

When you create an illustration from scratch, at times you may need different textures for surfaces or backgrounds. If you don't have images of surface textures available, you can create your own. Following are techniques for creating wood-grain textures. An advantage to making your own textures is that you can customize them. Each time you create a texture, it will look slightly different because the filters don't give the exact same result twice. Be sure to make your texture files larger than needed so that you can copy and paste different parts of them as needed. Also, save the files for reuse. Also included are some tips on how to recolor the textures, to reuse them for other projects. If you're interested in other organic and synthetic textures, see "Stone and Stucco Textures" on page 72.

Wood-grain texture

1   Create a new file larger than the size of the wood surface you will use. (This allows room for cropping out areas you may not want to use.) Double-click the Background layer and rename it Wood Base.

Converting the Background layer to a regular layer saves you a step because you will need a layer filled with white that can have a layer effect applied to it. You can't apply layer effects to Background layers.

2   Press the D key to return the foreground and background colors to their defaults. Choose Filter > Render > Fibers. Use the following values to create a soft, textured base: Variance = 1 and Strength = 1.

Creating different wood colors

Follow the Wood-grain Textures technique to create a rich, red wood grain. Then use the following values to get the colors shown in these examples.

Change overlay color for Wood Base layer to R = 250, G = 249, B = 146

Set Wood Grain layer mode to Color Burn

Set Wood Grain layer mode to Multiply and Opacity to 40%

Set Wood Grain layer mode to Exclusion and Opacity to 70%

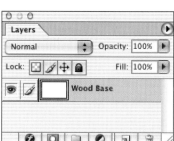

Change the Background layer to the Wood Base layer

Apply the Fibers filter

3 To colorize the texture, click the Add Layer Style button at the bottom of the Layers palette and choose the Color Overlay effect. In the Layer Style dialog box, set the Blend Mode to Linear Burn. Click the color swatch to display the color picker. Enter your own values or, to duplicate the example, enter these values: R = 210, G = 177, and B = 90. Click OK to apply the effect.

Apply the Color Overlay effect

4 Display the Color palette and change the foreground color using the following values: R = 189, G = 131, and B = 43. Change the background color using the following values: R = 218, G = 173, and B = 39.

You need to change the foreground and background colors so that the Fibers filter, which you'll use in step 6, will render the texture using these colors. The Fibers filter requires a fill; it won't work on a transparent layer.

5   Create a new layer in the Layers palette and name it Wood Grain. Set its mode to Linear Burn. Click OK. Press Option/ Alt+Delete/Backspace to fill the layer with the foreground color.

The texture color should now be a reddish brown.

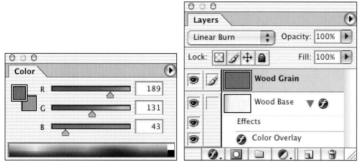

Change the foreground and background colors

Fill the Wood Grain layer with the foreground color

6   Choose Filter > Render > Fibers. Use the following values to create a wood grain texture: Variance = 7 and Strength = 52. Don't worry about the preview colors not matching your image. The preview in the Fibers dialog box shows the texture effect using the foreground and background colors; it will not preview any layer modes or effects. Click OK.

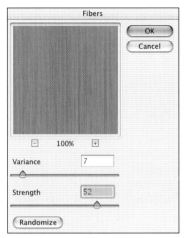

Apply the Fibers filter

7   Evaluate the look of the wood grain so far. If you like it, skip to step 9. If you want to try making a different wood grain texture, continue with step 8.

Evaluate the Wood Grain effect

8   If you want a different grain effect, choose Filter > Render > Fibers. (The shortcut for displaying the last filter used is Command/Ctrl+Option/Alt+F.) Click the Randomize button until you see a texture that you like. Click OK.

Reapply the Fibers filter for a different grain effect

9 To add some darker grain shadows, create a new layer by Option/Alt-clicking the New Layer button at the bottom of the Layers palette. Name the layer Grain Shadows. Choose the Multiply mode and select the Fill with Multiply-Neutral Color (White) option. Name the layer Grain Shadows and click OK.

You must fill this layer because you will apply the Fibers filter to it in the next step. The Multiply-Neutral Color option fills the layer with white.

10 Press the D key to return the foreground and background colors to their defaults. Choose Filter > Render > Fibers. Use the following values: Variance = 1 and Strength = 52. Click the Randomize button until the image is mostly white with a few light gray streaks. Click OK.

Keep the texture light. If you use too much texture on this layer, it will overpower the image with too much dark grain.

Duplicating the shadow grain

The Wood-grain Textures technique shows how to create a dark grain shadow layer. If you want to increase the grain or reposition it, follow these steps:

1 Create the wood grain by following steps 1 through 11 of the Wood-grain Textures technique.

2 Duplicate the Grain Shadow layer by dragging it to the New Layer button at the bottom of the Layers palette.

3 Choose Edit > Free Transform. Rotate the duplicate layer 180°. The rotation ensures that the extra grain shadow will fall in a different place instead of just darkening the existing grain shadow.

4 Continue with step 12 of the Wood-grain Textures technique.

One layer of grain shadow

Two layers of grain shadow

Creating different shadow grain

You can create a dark grain shadow layer using the same texture as the Wood Grain layer. To use a different kind of dark texture on the wood grain, follow the Wood-grain Textures technique, but for step 10, use the values shown here.

Choose Filter > Noise > Add Noise. Choose Monochrome with Amount = 30%. Then choose Filter > Noise > Median. Use a Radius of 1 pixel.

Choose Filter > Noise > Add Noise. Choose Monochrome with Amount = 30%. Then choose Filter > Texture > Grain. Use these values: Grain Type = Vertical, Intensity = 40, and Contrast = 50.

Complete step 10 as directed. Then select the Shadow Grain layer and choose Filter > Stylize > Diffuse. Choose Darken Only and click OK.

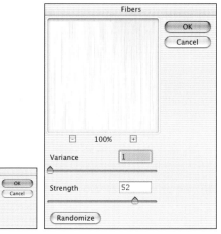

Create the Grain Shadows layer   *Apply the Fibers filter*

11 If the grain shadows seem too subtle, darken them by choosing Image > Adjustments > Levels. Move the black Input Levels slider to the right until the shadow grain is dark enough for your liking. Click OK.

12 Evaluate the effect. If you want to use the wood texture in another file, you must combine all the layers onto one layer. To combine the layers, create a new layer and name it Merged Wood. Move it to the top of the list in the Layers palette. With the Merged Wood layer selected, press Option/Alt (to keep the original layers intact) and choose Merge Visible from the Layers palette menu. You can now copy or transform the wood texture as desired.

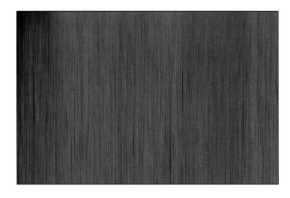

Wavy wood-grain textures

Some wood is fine-grained, like the example created with the Wood-Grain Texture technique. Some woods have an undulating pattern to the grain. You can simulate this with the Liquify filter. Depending on the tool you use, you can create soft, subtle curved grain or small, tight wavy grain.

1   Follow the Wood-grain Textures technique to create a fine-grained wood.

2   Duplicate the Merged Wood layer by Option/Alt-dragging it onto the New Layer button at the bottom of the Layers palette. Name the new layer Wavy Grain.

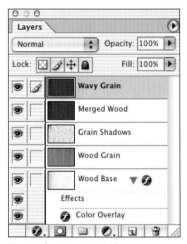

Create the Wavy Grain layer

3   With the Wavy Grain layer selected, choose Filter > Liquify. Use one of the following options.

   • Select the forward warp tool (the top left tool) and choose a very large brush size. For a smooth, elongated grain, use long, gentle strokes to change the grain.

   • Select the turbulence tool (eighth down from the top left) and choose a small brush. Click and hold down the mouse button over areas to make small waves.

Repairing blank spots

Using the Liquify filter to create waves in wood grain works great. But if you get too close to the edge, blank areas may start to enter the picture. You can fix the blanks by clicking with whatever tool you are using and gently nudging the image back up to cover the blank areas.

Edge of wood grain needs repair

Use brush to move image up

• Select the twirl clockwise tool (third from the top left) and choose a small brush. Make long smooth strokes to create bends in the grain.

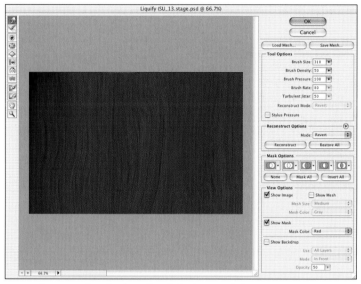

Forward warp tool with a large brush for long, undulating grain

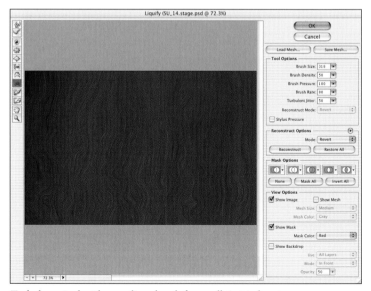

Turbulence tool with a medium brush for small, twisted grain

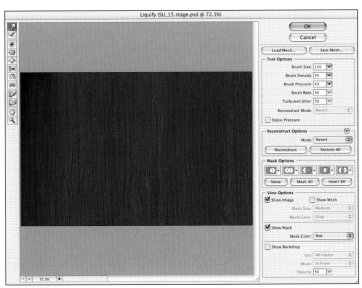

Twirl clockwise tool with a smaller brush for bends in the grain

Creating paper

Make a paper texture and then place it over your image so it looks as if it was painted on a textured paper. This texture works best on light images.

1   Press the D key to reset the default foreground and background colors.

2   Option/Alt-click the New Layer button at the bottom of the Layers palette. Choose Multiply mode and select the Fill with Multiply-Neutral Color option. Click OK.

3   Choose Filter > Sketch > Note Paper. Use these settings: Image Balance = 10, Graininess = 5, and Relief = 4. Click OK.

4   For a mottled paper look, Option/Alt-click the New Layer button at the bottom of the Layers palette. Choose Overlay mode and select the Fill with Overlay-Neutral Color option. Click OK.

5   Choose Filter > Render > Clouds. Set the opacity for the layer at 50%. Position the Clouds layer under the Texture layer.

Section 2 | Drawing

11 | Reverse-shape graphics

Create an art deco look by reversing the colors of overlapping shapes. This is easy to do with shape layers. Shape layers are solid-color layers with vector masks. Here are three different methods to reverse shapes. First, simply reverse one shape out of another. Second, use a second color to show through the hole created when you reverse the shape. Third, reverse type out of a shape. Remember, a shape layer can have multiple shapes; wherever shapes overlap, a reverse will occur.

One-color reverse shapes

1   Create a new shape layer. Do this by selecting a shape tool in the toolbox. Use the tooltips to help you identify the tool you want. In the tool options bar, select the Shape Layers option. Then draw the shape with the shape tool. The following example used a custom shape.

Create a shape layer

2   To add a shape or path to the shape layer and create a reverse effect, select any shape tool from the tool options bar. With the shape layer created in step 1 still selected, click the Exclude Overlapping Shape Areas button in the tool options bar. Use the tooltips to help you identify the option you want. Draw the shape so that it intersects the existing shape on the layer. In the following example, the pen tool was used to create the new shape. If you are satisfied with the effect, save the file.

Creating preset custom shapes

You can make and save your own library of shapes to use in Photoshop. Follow these steps:

1   Select the pen tool or one of the shape tools in the toolbox. In the tool options bar, select the Paths option. Use the tool to create a path.

2   Select the path selection tool in the toolbox. Click the path or shape to select it.

Selected path

3   Choose Edit > Define Custom Shape. Name the shape and click OK.

4   To use the shape, select the custom shape tool in the toolbox. Select the shape in the Shape pop-up palette in the tool options bar.

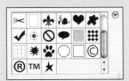

Shape pop-up palette

5   To save the custom shape as part of a library, select Save Shapes from the pop-up palette menu.

Changing a shape layer's color

When you create a shape layer, it automatically adopts the foreground color as its base color. You can change the color of a shape layer one of two ways. Select the shape layer and do one of the following:

- Click the color swatch in the tool options bar. The color swatch appears in the options bar only if a shape tool and the Shape Layers option in the option bar are selected. When the color picker appears, select a new color and click OK.
- Double-click the shape layer thumbnail in the Layers palette to open the color picker. Select a new color and click OK.

Use a shape or pen tool to add to the shape layer

Two-color reverse shapes

1   Create a new shape layer. Do this by selecting a shape tool in the toolbox. In the tool options bar, select the Shape layers option. Then draw the shape with the shape tool. In the Layers palette, name the layer Shape 1.

To make your own custom shapes, see "Creating preset custom shapes" on page 97.

Create the Shape 1 layer

2   Click the Shape Layers button in the tool options palette. Then draw a new shape to create a second shape layer. Change the color of the new shape layer by clicking the color swatch in the tool options bar. In the Layers palette,

move the new shape layer below the Shape 1 layer. Name the new layer Shape 2.

The Shape 2 layer will fill in the "holes" that are created when you combine the two shapes in step 5.

Create the Shape 2 layer

3   Select the path selection tool in the toolbox. Using the tool, click the edge of the path on the Shape 2 layer to select it. Choose Edit > Copy to copy the path.

4   In the Layers palette, click the Shape 1 layer vector thumbnail and choose Edit > Paste. The path will be added to the existing path on that shape layer.

The default setting for the way the overlapping shapes interact is Add to Shape Area. You will change this in the next step.

Paste the path into the Shape 1 layer

Selecting and copying shapes or paths

It's useful to know that you can select a path two different ways. You can also copy a path in two ways. Each way has a different advantage. Choose the method that suits your purposes.

First, select a path in one of these ways:

- To select all paths on a shape layer, click the vector mask thumbnail in the Layers palette.
- To select an individual path on a shape layer, click the vector mask thumbnail to display the paths. Select the path selection tool in the toolbox. Click the edge of the path you want to select. Notice that the edge and the anchor points are highlighted.

Once the path is selected, choose Edit > Copy and then paste it in one of these ways:

- To create a work path, select a layer (if it is a shape layer, first make sure that the vector mask is deselected), and choose Edit > Paste. Display the Paths palette to view the work path. Save and name it if desired.
- To add a path to another shape layer, select the shape layer in the Layers palette and click its vector mask thumbnail. Make sure that the vector mask is selected (it toggles on and off). Choose Edit > Paste to add the path to the vector mask.

Creating precise shapes

Sometimes you need a precisely sized circle or square for your image. Making shapes in a specified size is easy with the shape tools.

1. Select the shape tool you want to use.
2. Display the Geometry Options pop-up palette in the tool options bar.
3. To create a specific size, select the Fixed Size option. Enter a value for both width and height. Press Return/Enter to close the palette.
4. Use the tool to draw the shape. When you are ready to draw a different size, repeat steps 1 through 3.

Geometry Options palette for the ellipse tool.

5. With the path still selected, click the Exclude Overlapping Areas button in the tool options bar. A hole now appears where the shapes overlap that lets the color on the Shape 2 layer show through. Save the file.

Select the Exclude Overlapping Areas option

Type reverse shapes

1. Follow step 1 of the Two-color Reverse Shapes technique.
2. Create a type layer with a different color. Make sure that the type overlaps the shape on the Shape 1 layer. In the Layers palette, move the type layer below the Shape 1 layer.

Create the Shape 1 layer

3. In the Layers palette, duplicate the type layer by dragging its thumbnail to the New Layer button.

4   With the duplicate type layer still selected, convert the type
    to shapes by choosing Layer > Type > Convert to Shape.
    Choose Edit > Copy to copy the type shapes.

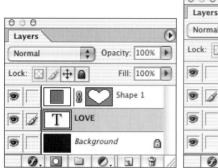

Create a type layer

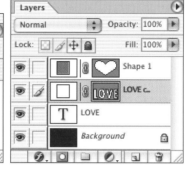

Convert duplicate type layer to shapes

5   Follow steps 3 through 5 of the Two-color Reverse Shapes
    technique, substituting the type shapes layer for the Shape 2
    layer in the instructions. Save the file.

To get a one-color effect, hide both the type layer and the type
shapes layer.

Type shapes reversed

12 | Shaded spheres

Common Chemical Compounds

Compound	Name	Molecule model
H_2O	Water	
NH_3	Ammonia	
H_2O_2	Hydrogen Peroxide	
CO_2	Carbon Dioxide	

Here are two different ways to make spheres in Photoshop—using gradients or layer styles. Using the gradient fill tool, you can create shaded spheres. Gradients let you position the highlight wherever you want; you can create many spheres of varying sizes with the same gradient. The disadvantage is that each time you want to change the color of your sphere you must make a new gradient. The second technique uses layer styles. Once created, a layer style can be used over and over to create all different colored spheres. The disadvantages to this method are that you can only have the highlight in the center and you may have to adjust the settings for spheres of different sizes.

Gradient spheres

1   Open a new or existing file and create a new layer. Name the layer Sphere.

2   Select the elliptical marquee tool. Press Shift and draw a circle.

To draw the circle from the center point, press Option/Alt as you start to draw.

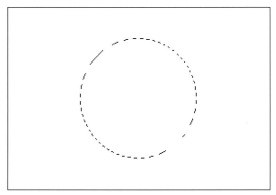

Make an elliptical selection

3   Select the gradient tool in the toolbox. Then click the Radial Gradient button in the tool options bar.

4   Click the gradient sample to display the Gradient Editor dialog box. Use a highlight color at one end and a shadow color at the opposite end. Place a solid color at the 50% point on the gradient slider. Click the stop, and then click the Color swatch in the Stops section to change the colors. Name the gradient Sphere and click New to save it as a Preset. Click OK.

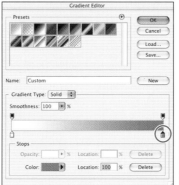
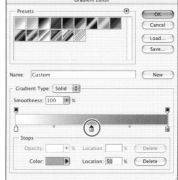

Create the shadow-color stop   *Create the middle solid-color stop*

5   Select the Sphere gradient in the Gradient pop-up palette. Position the radial gradient tool inside the circle selection at the point where you want the highlight. Drag to the edge of the selection and release the mouse button. Deselect the sphere.

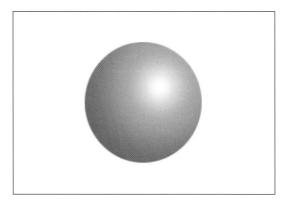

Completed gradient sphere

Layer-style spheres

1   Open a new or existing file and create a new layer. Name the layer Sphere.

2   Select the elliptical marquee tool. Press Shift and draw a circle. Choose a color from the Color palette and fill the selection with that color. Deselect the circle.

Draw and color a circle

3   Click the Add Layer Style button in the Layers palette and select Inner Shadow. With the Preview box checked, adjust the Distance and Size settings until your sphere looks like the example. The amounts will vary depending on the sphere's size and resolution. In this example, Distance = 11 px, Size = 54 px, and the angle = −164° at a resolution of 144 ppi. Don't click OK yet.

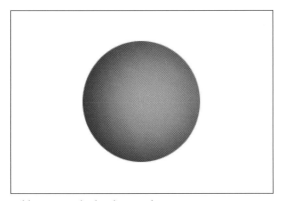

Add an Inner Shadow layer style

Converting unit values on the fly

You don't have to do the math to convert from pixels to points or from inches to centimeters, and you don't have to change your preferences. Let Photoshop convert values for you. When you enter a value in the tool options bar, you can follow that number with any of several abbreviations for units of measurement. For example, if you know the height should be 2 inches and the width should be 150 pixels, you can enter "2 in" for height and "150 px" for width. Following are the abbreviations that Photoshop recognizes:

Pixels	px, pixel
Inches	in, inch
Centimeters	cm, centimeter
Millimeters	mm, millimeter
Picas	picas
Percent	pct, percent, %

Shortcut: Open a layer effect with context menus

Another way to access or add a layer effect is to use the context menus. Control-click (Mac OS X) or right mouse button-click (Windows) a layer effect name in the Layers palette. Select the new layer effect you want and release the mouse button.

4 With the Layer Style dialog box still open, click the arrow next to the contour in the Quality section to display the Contour pop-up palette. Select the Gaussian contour. (Hold the pointer over a contour thumbnail and its name will appear.) Click the Layer Style dialog box to close the pop-up palette. Do not click OK yet.

5 From the Styles list, click the name Inner Glow to apply the effect and display its options. Click the color swatch to open the color picker. Change the glow color to white and click OK. Set the Technique to Precise and the Source to Center. Adjust the Size amount until you have a white highlight in the center of your sphere.

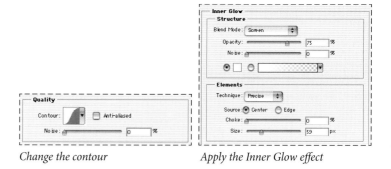

Change the contour   *Apply the Inner Glow effect*

6 Vary settings depending on the diameter and resolution of your sphere. For this example, the Inner Glow size was set to 59 px. When you are satisfied with the effect, click OK.

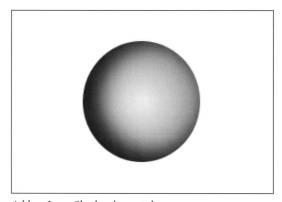

Add an Inner Shadow layer style

7   If the shading and highlights have flattened the color in the sphere, you can adjust for this. From the Layers palette menu, choose Duplicate Layer to duplicate the Sphere layer. Click OK.

8   Remove the effects from the Sphere Copy layer by dragging its Effects sublayer to the Trash button at the bottom of the Layers palette. Change the layer blending mode to Soft Light. Adjust the opacity if necessary. If the gradient is banded, you may need to change colors.

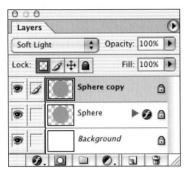

Set the blending mode to Soft Light

9   To change the color of the sphere quickly, turn on the Lock Transparent Pixels option for the Sphere and Sphere copy layers. Then choose different colors and fill the layers until you are satisfied with the result. Remember, you will need to change the color of both the Sphere layer and the duplicate you made in step 7.

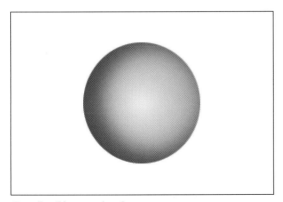

Completed layer-style sphere

Colorizing without repainting

If you want to change the color of a sphere without repainting it and its corresponding layers, try using an adjustment layer. In this example, a Hue/Saturation layer was added and the hue value was changed to alter the sphere color.

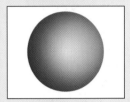

Original sphere

Adjustment layer added

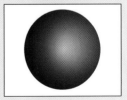

Result

13 | Perspective grids

You can create a perspective grid in Photoshop that helps you match the perspective of imported graphics and images to that of the background image. This technique is especially helpful with images that contain strong perspective lines. To create the grid, you draw paths that define the vanishing points and horizon line of the image. Then you draw grid lines for positioning and sizing the imported artwork. (Don't worry if the guidelines reach outside of the image; the pen tool displays outside the image in Full Screen mode.) Once the grid is created, you distort the imported image to align it with the grid lines.

1 Open a background file.

Background file

2 Option/Alt-click the New Layer button at the bottom of the Layers palette and name the layer Guidelines.

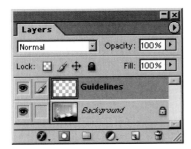

Create the Guidelines layer

Converting the Background layer

Because you can't use layer modes or transparency with the Background layer, sometimes you may want to convert your Background layer into a regular layer. Or you may want to use a different layer as a Background layer. Here's how to convert it.

- To make the Background layer into a regular layer, simply double-click the Background layer thumbnail in the Layers palette. When the New Layer dialog box opens, name the layer and click OK.

- To convert a regular layer into a Background layer, first make sure that the image doesn't already have a Background layer. An image cannot have two Background layers; if one already exists, follow the preceding directions to convert it to a regular layer. Select the layer you want to be the new Background layer. Choose Layer > New > Background From Layer.

Changing the workspace background color

When you choose the display option Full Screen Mode with Menu Bar, the area surrounding the image is a medium gray. You can change this color to view more easily the guidelines that extend outside the image. Select the paint bucket tool in the toolbox (it's hidden under the gradient tool). Select a color in the Color palette, and then position the paint bucket over the gray area. Shift-click to fill the area with a new color. In Full Screen mode, you cannot change the workspace color. It will always be black.

3   Select the pen tool in the toolbox. Click the Paths button in the tool options bar. Select the Full Screen Mode with Menu Bar button at the bottom of the toolbox. Zoom out and draw two paths that follow the perspective lines in your image. Use the direct selection tool to extend the endpoints of the lines to a point where they intersect. This is referred to as a vanishing point.

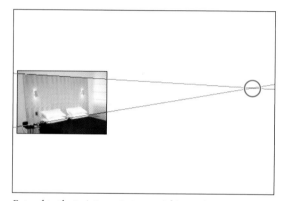

Extend paths to intersect at a vanishing point

4   Create the first point of a new line, hold down Shift, and click the second point to draw a horizontal line. Use the direct selection tool to move the horizontal line until it intersects the vanishing point.

This is the horizon line. Depending on the angle and size of your image, it may not appear inside of the image area.

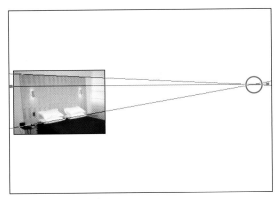

Create the horizon line

5 Draw additional guidelines to help create the perspective for positioning additional images or graphics.

This example shows additional lines drawn as guides for a painting that will be placed on the headboard.

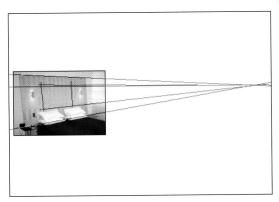

Create additional lines for positioning

6 Select the work path, if it is not already selected, in the Paths palette, and then choose Save Path from the palette menu. Name the path Perspective Grid.

Shortcut: Zoom from the keyboard

You can access the zoom tool with the keyboard at any time. This shortcut is handy when you want to compare the image with a preview in a filter dialog box. Here are shortcuts for getting the zoom tool:

- Move the cursor over an area in the image you want to zoom in on. To zoom in, press Command/Ctrl to change the pointer to the zoom tool, and click the mouse button. To zoom out, press Command/Ctrl+Option/Alt and click the mouse button.
- Press Command/Ctrl+ − [minus key] to zoom out. To zoom in, press Command/Ctrl+ = [equal key], and click the mouse button.
- Press Command/Ctrl+0, and click the mouse button to fit the image on the screen.
- Press Option/Alt+ Command/Ctrl+0 to view the actual pixel size of the image.

Shortcut: Select a specific layer

Context menus can help you select the layer on which you want to work by displaying an image's layers. Using context menus is especially helpful when you have a file with multiple layers and you do not know on which layer an object resides.

1 Select the move tool:
   • In the toolbox;
   • By pressing Command/Ctrl; or
   • By pressing and releasing the V key
2 Position the pointer over the image or object on which you want to work. Control-click (Mac OS X) or right mouse-click (Windows) to display the context menu. Where you click, a list with all layers that contain pixels will appear.

Context menu reveals layers with objects where you click the mouse

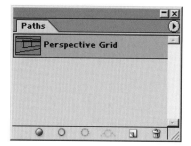

Save the path as Perspective Grid

7 Select the pencil tool in the toolbox. Choose Window > Brushes to display the Brushes palette. Select the Hard Round 1 pixel brush.

8 Choose Window > Color to display the Color palette. Select a very bright color to stroke the guidelines. Choose a color that will show up well against your image.

The guidelines will not print; they serve only as references while building the image.

9 Make sure that the Guidelines layer in the Layers palette is selected. With the Perspective Grid path still selected, choose Stroke Path from the Paths palette menu. Make sure that the pencil tool is the selected tool, and click OK.

Stroke the path with the pencil

10 In the Paths palette, click the blank area below the Perspective Grid path to deselect the paths. If the lines don't show up well on your image, continue with step 11. If the lines show up well, skip to step 12.

Check grid lines for contrast and visibility

11 Select a new color in the Color palette. Turn on the Lock Transparent Pixels option for the Guidelines layer. Choose Edit > Fill, and fill the layer with the new foreground color. Continue trying this until you find a color that contrasts well with your image.

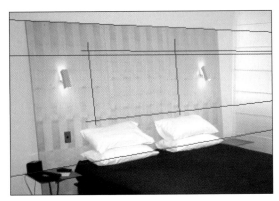

Change guidelines color

12 Create, place, or paste the image to be transformed into perspective.

Centering a selection with drag and drop

Dragging or dropping images or selections from other files creates a new layer. If you want that selection to be centered when you drag it into the new file, follow these steps:

1　Select the area you want to drag into another file. If the whole layer is to be dragged, no selection is needed.

2　Select the move tool.

3　Shift-drag the layer or selection into the window of the new file.

Why is that pasted image so big?

When you paste or drag and drop a new image into a file, the new image adopts the resolution of the file in which you place it. In some cases, the resolution may differ from its original file resolution and result in a size change. If you don't want such a surprise, make sure that the resolution of both files is the same before you copy and paste or drag and drop. (Use the Image Size command to check the file resolution.) If the resolutions don't match, you will have to scale the object, which can compromise the image quality.

Paste or place the image to be transformed

13 Choose Edit > Free Transform. To distort freely, press the Command/Ctrl key as you drag one of the corner points to its desired location. Use the guidelines as reference to position each of the corner points of the Transform bounding box. Once the image has been scaled and distorted to fit the guidelines, press Return/Enter to apply the transformation.

Use Free Transform with the guidelines to distort the image

14 Hide or delete the Guidelines layer. If necessary, adjust the layer blending mode or opacity of the transformed image to make it fit visually with the Background layer. Repeat steps 5 through 14 for any other objects that you add to the image.

Hide the guidelines

Removing perspective distortion with the crop tool

You may want to remove a perspective distortion rather than introduce one. These distortions are common in photographs of buildings or other objects with rectangular planes that were photographed from an angle. You can use the crop tool to correct the problem. Note that this correction only works on images that contain a rectangular object.

1   Select the crop tool in the toolbox, and roughly select the area to be cropped and corrected. The selection doesn't have to be perfect because you will adjust it in step 3.

2   In the tool options bar, select the Perspective option.

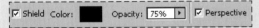

Select the Perspective option in the tool options bar

3   Move the corners until they align with the edges of the object that you want to make rectangular. These edges will become perpendicular after the crop.

4   Press Return/Enter to complete the action. Notice that the edges of the cropping area are now perpendicular to the edge of the image.

Before perspective crop   *After perspective crop*

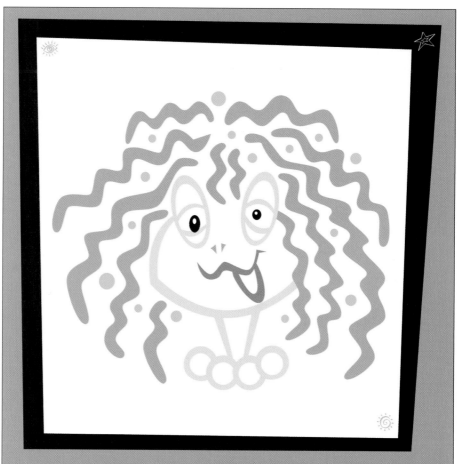

I was going to have cosmetic surgery until I noticed that the doctor's office was full of portraits by Picasso. — Rita Rudner

You can bring clip art into Photoshop several ways. Most digital clip art is saved in EPS format. That means it is created with paths in a drawing program like Illustrator. If you have Illustrator, you can open the clip art file, sort the shape into layers, and then export the art as a PSD file so that it will be easy to open and use in Photoshop. If you don't have Illustrator, you can place the art directly into Photoshop, but you won't be able to use the paths. Photoshop will rasterize the file when you place it. Following are the two respective techniques on how to get clip art into your Photoshop file and then colorize the art.

Placed EPS art with black outlines

If your clip art is black-and-white EPS art with black outlines and you don't want to open it in Illustrator, use this technique. You will place the art in Photoshop and create new layers with colors to fill in the white spaces.

1   Choose File > Place. Navigate to the clip art file you want, and click Place. Scale and position the art and then press Return/Enter to rasterize it on a new layer.

Place the clip art in your file

2   Double-click the layer name in the Layers palette. Name the layer Black Outlines. Set the blending mode to Multiply. Click the Lock All button.

Using fonts as clip art

Loads of fonts can be used as clip art. Sometimes they are called dingbats, pi fonts, ornaments, borders, or mini-pictures. To use a font as clip art, simply follow these steps:

1   Create some type with a dingbat font. To access the font outlines, choose Type > Convert to Shape.

2   Change the color of the shape layer, if desired.

Convert type to shape layer

3   Duplicate the shape layer by dragging it onto the New Layer button at the bottom of the Layers palette.

4   Double-click the shape layer thumbnail and change the color of the new shape layer.

5   Use the direct selection tool and select the shapes on the shape layer that you don't want filled with a new color. Delete them by pressing Delete/Backspace.

Delete unwanted shapes

Locking layers

A layer can be locked four different ways. At the top of the Layers palette, just under the blending mode pop-up menu, are four lock buttons.

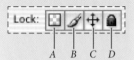

A **Lock Transparency** protects all the transparent pixels on a layer and lets you change any solid or semi-transparent pixels.

B **Lock Image** prevents you from changing the pixels on a layer with the painting tools.

C **Lock Position** prevents you from moving the pixels on a layer.

D **Lock All** locks the transparency, image, and position of a layer.

Locking the Black Outlines layer lets you select pixels on that layer but not paint over them. You will need to protect this layer when you start painting in step 6.

3   Option/Alt-click the New Layer button at the bottom of the Layers palette to create a new layer. Name the layer Colors and click OK. Move the Colors layer below the Black Outlines layer in the Layers palette.

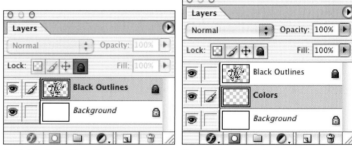

Lock Black Outlines layer   *Create the Colors layer*

4   Select the magic wand tool in the toolbox. In the tool options bar, set the tolerance to 254 and turn on Anti-alised and Contiguous.

Setting the tolerance to 254 will spread the selections into the black outline area and ensure that no gap appears between the outlines and the color fills.

Set the Tolerance to 254

5   In the Layers palette, select the Black Outlines layer. With the magic wand tool, click an area that you want to fill with color. If you have several areas you want to fill with the same color, Shift-click until they are all selected. Don't fill with color yet.

6   Before you fill with color, select the Colors layer in the Layers palette. This is very important, because nothing will happen if you try to fill the selection with color on the locked Black Outlines layer. Select a color in the Colors palette and press Option/Alt+Delete/Backspace to fill the selection with the foreground color.

Fill the selection with the foreground color

7 Deselect and repeat steps 5 and 6 for each different color you want to use.

8 When you have finished adding color, save the file. If you need the clip art on one layer, select the Black Outlines layer in the Layers palette, unlock it, and then choose Merge Down from the Layers palette menu.

Completed colorized clip art

Copying paths from Illustrator to Photoshop

If your clip art is prepainted with color, not outlined in black, or if you just want to change the paths or artwork, use this method. This method of copying paths also places each color on a different layer. So if you will use the artwork several times in different color ways, this is the best technique for you. You'll copy the clip art paths in Illustrator, and then paste them as paths in Photoshop. Then you'll organize and build the file as you colorize.

1   Open the clip art file in Illustrator. Choose Illustrator > Preferences > File Handling & Clipboard (Mac OS X) or Edit > Preferences > File Handling & Clipboard (Windows). Choose Copy As AICB and select the Preserve Paths option. Click OK.

Open the clip art file in Illustrator

2   Choose Select > All, and then choose Edit > Copy to copy the clip art paths to the clipboard.

3   Launch Photoshop and open the file to which you will add clip art, or open a new file.

4   Choose Edit > Paste. When the Paste dialog box appears, select the Path option and click OK.

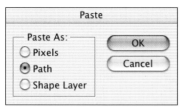

Choose Paste As Path

5 While the paths are visible, adjust the size and position. Choose Edit > Free Transform Path. Transform the clip art to the desired size, rotation, and position; then press Return/Enter to complete the transformations. The following example shows the size reduced.

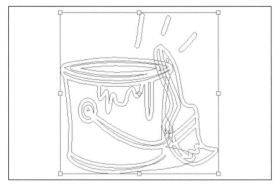

Scale the paths to desired size

6 Display the Paths palette. Double-click the Work Path name to save and name the path. Name it Clip Art Paths. Click OK.

7 Create a new layer in the Layers palette. Name it Black Outlines.

EPS clip art is often created by autotracing hand-drawn art. This autotracing results in files with black shapes behind white or colored shapes, instead of actual outlines as in the following example. Thus, it is easier to build the file with the black shapes on the bottom layer.

Pasting paths as shape layers

If you're making one- or two-color clip art, it's best to paste paths as shape layers. Follow these steps:

1 Open the clip art file in Illustrator. Select the shapes that will be one color. In this example, they'll be black. Choose Edit > Copy.

2 Switch to Photoshop and choose Edit > Paste. Select the Shape Layer option and click OK.

3 Change the foreground color and repeat steps 1 and 2 for the remaining shapes. You may need to adjust the position of the second set of paths. Press Command/Ctrl to get the move tool, and move the paths to align the shapes.

In the example here, because the paintbrush needed to be in front of the paint can, a second shape layer was created.

Clip Art shape layers

Shortcut: Load a path as a selection

Quickly create a selection from a path by Command/Ctrl-clicking its thumbnail. This works in the Paths palette as well as in the Layers palette. Click a shape layer. Then Command/Ctrl-click the vector mask thumbnail to load it as a selection. (If you are not sure which is the vector mask thumbnail, position the pointer over a thumbnail to display its name.)

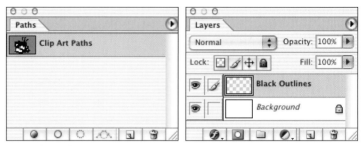

Name the path   *Create the Black Outlines layer*

8 Choose the path selection tool in the toolbox. Shift-click to select the shapes you want to fill with black. When they are selected, click the Load Path as a Selection button at the bottom of the Paths palette.

9 Press the D key to return the foreground and background colors to their defaults. Make sure that the Black Outlines layer is selected in the Layers palette and press Option/Alt+Delete/Backspace to fill the selection with black.

Fill the selection with black

10 Create a new layer in the Layers palette. Name it after the color shapes you will paint next—for example, Gold Shapes.

11 With the path selection tool, Shift-click to select the shapes you want to fill with the next color. When they are selected, click the Load Path as a Selection button at the bottom of the Paths palette.

12 In the Color palette, select a new color. Make sure that the new color layer is selected in the Layers palette, and press Option/Alt+Delete/Backspace to fill the selection with the foreground color.

Fill the selection with a color

13 Repeat steps 10 through 12 for each color in the illustration. When you are satisfied with the results, save the file. To change a color quickly in one of the color layers, select the layer and turn on the Lock Transparent Pixels option in the Layers palette. Choose a new color and fill the layer by pressing Option/Alt+Delete/Backspace. By locking the transparent pixels, you fill only the areas that contain color.

In some cases you may need to reposition some of the layers to prevent unwanted overlaps. In the following example, the paintbrush shapes had to be moved above the paint can shapes.

Shortcut: Hide path edges

Sometimes the path outlines can be distracting once you've made a selection from them. To hide them from view so that only the marquee selection edges appear, click in the Paths palette in the empty space below the paths. All visible paths will become invisible. To redisplay the path outlines, click the path name.

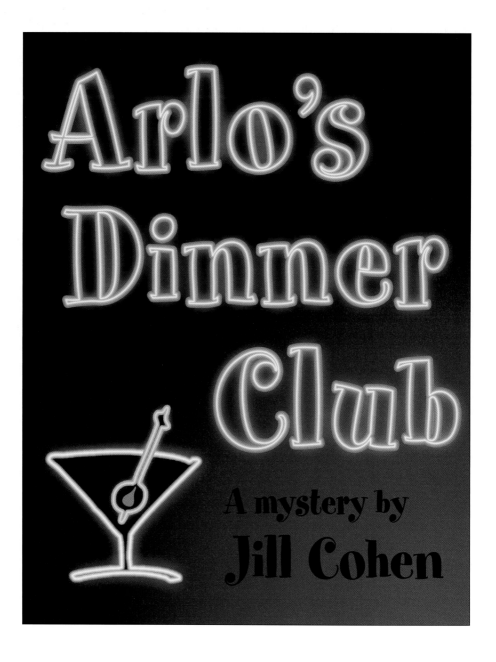

Making graphics glow in Photoshop is easy, but making digital neon is a different matter. Real neon signs and graphics are made from colored tubes filled with gas. The tubes are the same width and are wrapped and twisted to make shapes and letterforms. To make digital neon, use type or shapes created in either Illustrator or Photoshop. Then create a special neon gradient that you will apply as a layer style to the graphic or type. The layer style will outline the shapes with the digital neon tubing. Finally, add a glow to make the neon appear to emit a halo of colored light.

1   Create a new file and fill the Background layer with a dark color.

2   Add the graphic that will become a neon graphic by either making a type layer or using the pen tool and making a shape layer. Don't worry about the graphic's fill color. It will be changed in a later step.

You can also make a shape layer by copying and pasting a graphic from Illustrator.

Note: If you want to vary the colored neon for different shapes, put each differently colored shape onto a different layer. Everything on one layer will have the same color neon.

What typefaces work well with neon outlines?

- Sans serif
- Bold, heavy, or black styles
- Simple designs

What typefaces *don't* work well as neon outlines?

- Ornate script faces
- Light, thin, or condensed styles
- Highly stylized or illustrative designs
- Faces with delicate serifs

Create type or a graphic on a separate layer

Sampling colors for your gradient

There are several ways to sample colors when creating a gradient in the Gradient Editor. First, select the color stop you want to change. Then do one of the following:

- Click the color swatch to open the color picker.
- Double-click the color stop to open the color picker.
- Move the pointer into the gradient bar to change it to the eyedropper. Click to sample a color from the gradient bar.
- Move the Gradient Editor dialog box so that the image is visible. Move the pointer into the image area and click to sample a color from the image.
- Display the Color palette before you open the Gradient Editor. After clicking the color stop in the Gradient Editor, move the pointer to the color ramp at the bottom of the Color palette and sample a color from it.
- Display the Swatches palette before you open the Gradient Editor. After clicking the color stop in the Gradient Editor, move the pointer to a swatch in the Swatches palette and sample a color.
- Choose either Foreground or Background from the Color pop-up menu in the Stops section of the Gradient Editor dialog box.

Neon gradients

Now you will create a gradient that will eventually appear as the neon tube gradient. Depending on the number of graphics you have, you may want to create more than one neon gradient.

1   Select the gradient tool in the toolbox. Click the gradient swatch in the tool options bar to open the Gradient Editor. Set the Gradient Type to Solid. To begin, select the Black, White gradient. Don't click OK yet.

2   Double-click the leftmost color stop (the black one) to change its color. When the color picker appears, select the color for the outside edges of your neon gradient. Click OK to close the color picker. Don't close the Gradient Editor yet.

3   To change the rightmost color stop (the white one) to the same color as the left color stop, click the right color stop once to select it. Move the pointer inside the gradient bar until the eyedropper tool appears. Move the eyedropper to the leftmost side of the gradient and click to select the same color you used for the left side of the gradient.

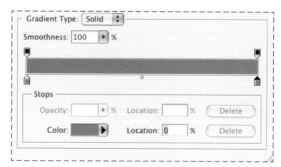

Set the right and left color stops to the same color

4   Click just below the gradient bar at its middle to add a new color stop. Drag it to the 50% location. Double-click the color stop or click once on the color swatch and change the color to white.

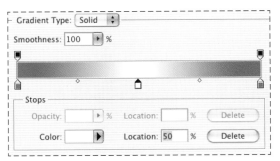

Set a white color stop at the 50% location

5   Create two more color stops on either side of the middle white color stop. Place one at the 35% location and one at the 65% location. Fill both stops with the same color. Choose a color that is lighter and brighter than the edge color.

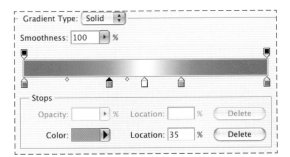

Set bright color stops on either side of the middle stop

6   Name the gradient and click New to add the gradient to the presets in the Gradient pop-up palette. Click OK.

Neon-outline layer styles

1   Select the first layer to which you will add neon outlines. At the bottom of the Layers palette, click the Add Layer Style button and choose Stroke.

2   Choose Center as the Position. Choose Gradient as the Fill Type. Click the gradient swatch and navigate to the gradient you created in step 6. Click OK. In the Layer Style dialog box, choose Shape Burst as the Style.

Using a stroke layer style

Adding a Stroke layer effect to your shape or type lets you choose from several variations, including three fill types. If you select the Gradient fill type, you can then choose from five gradient styles. Below are a few of the stroke options.

Color fill type

Gradient fill type, Linear style

Gradient fill type, Shape Burst style

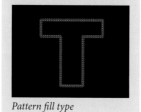

Pattern fill type

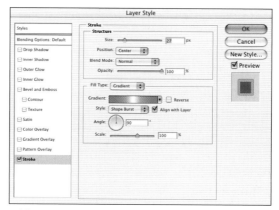

Add a Stroke layer style

3   Turn on the Preview option and move the Layer Style dialog box so that you can see the image. Adjust the size until you like the effect. The size will vary depending on the size of the graphic and its resolution. Do not click OK yet.

Adjust the size of the Stroke layer effect

4   Click the name Outer Glow in the list at the left side of the Layer Style dialog box to add an outer glow and display its options. Make sure that the Blend Mode is set to Screen. Click the color swatch and choose a color that is slightly lighter or brighter than the color on the outside edge of the stroke gradient. Set the Technique to Softer and adjust the size until you like the effect. Don't click OK yet.

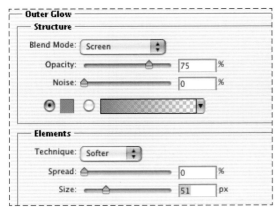

Add an Outer Glow layer effect

5 Click the name Inner Glow in the list on the left side of the
Layer Style dialog box to add an inner glow and display its
options. Click the color swatch and choose the same color
that you used for the outer glow. Set the Technique to Softer,
the Source to Edge and adjust the size until you like the
effect. The Blend Mode should be set to Screen. If you want
to leave the shapes filled with a solid color and outlined
with the neon stroke, skip to step 7. If you want to remove
the fill so that only the neon outline shows, continue
with step 6.

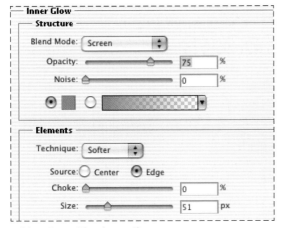

Add an Inner Glow layer effect

Result of the Outer and Inner Glow layer effects

6   To hide the shape's fill color so that only the neon stroke
    shows, click the name Blending Options in the list at the
    left side of the Layer Style dialog box. Set the Fill Opacity to
    0% and make sure that the Blend Interior Effects as Group
    option is deselected.

This step ensures that the fill color disappears and the inner
glow displays properly.

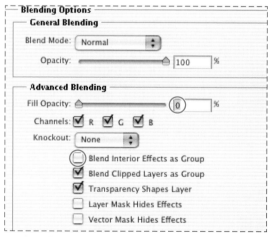

Set the Fill Opacity to 0%

7   If you have no other layers to add neon strokes to, save the
    file. If you want to save the style, drag the layer name from
    the Layers palette into the Styles palette. Name the style and

click OK. If you want to add different colored neon strokes to other layers, follow the steps in the next technique, "Multiple neon strokes."

Neon stroke remains after shape fill is removed

Multiple neon strokes

If you want to use several different-colored neon strokes in a file, you can copy the layer style and then simply apply a different color gradient to the stroke layer style. Here's how to do it.

1   Select a layer in the Layers palette that has the neon stroke layer style applied to it. Choose Layer > Layer Style > Copy Layer Style.

2   Now click the layer in the Layers palette to which you will apply a neon outline. Choose Layer > Layer Style > Paste Layer Style.

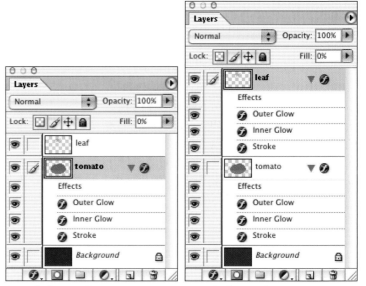

Copy the layer style   Paste the layer style

3   In the Layers palette, under the layer just pasted, double-
    click the Stroke layer style item. This opens the Layer Style
    dialog box. Click the gradient swatch to open the Gradient
    Editor. Follow the steps in the Neon Gradients technique
    and change the colors of the gradient for the new graphic
    shape. Click OK to close the Gradient Editor.

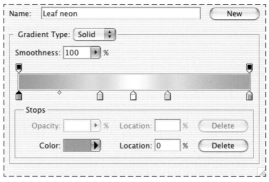

Change the colors and create a new neon gradient

4   Adjust the size of the stroke if necessary.

In this example, the size was reduced because the leaf shape is smaller and more complex than the tomato shape.

Reduced neon stroke size

5 Follow steps 4 through 7 of the Neon-Outline Layer Styles technique, changing the colors of the outer glow and inner glow to match the new gradient colors.

6 Repeat steps 1 through 4 of the Multiple Neon Strokes technique for as many layers as necessary. If you want to save the style, drag the layer name from the Layers palette into the Styles palette. Name the style and click OK.

This example shows the Blending options changed. In the Advanced Blending section of the Layer Styles dialog box, the Knockout was set to Shallow to block out the red neon that appeared inside the leaf shape.

Inner and Outer Glow colors are changed

Applying preset styles to layers

To apply a preset style to a layer, select the layer in the Layers palette and do one of the following:

- Display the Styles palette and click the style.
- Drag a style from the Styles palette onto the layer name in the Layers palette.
- Open the Layer Style dialog box by double-clicking the layer thumbnail in the Layers palette. On the left side of the Layer Style dialog box, click the word Styles at the top of the list. Click a style to apply it. Click OK.
- Hold down Shift while clicking a style in the Styles palette to add it to a style already applied to a layer. Simply clicking the style in the Styles palette will replace the style already applied to the selected layer.

16 Digital woodcuts

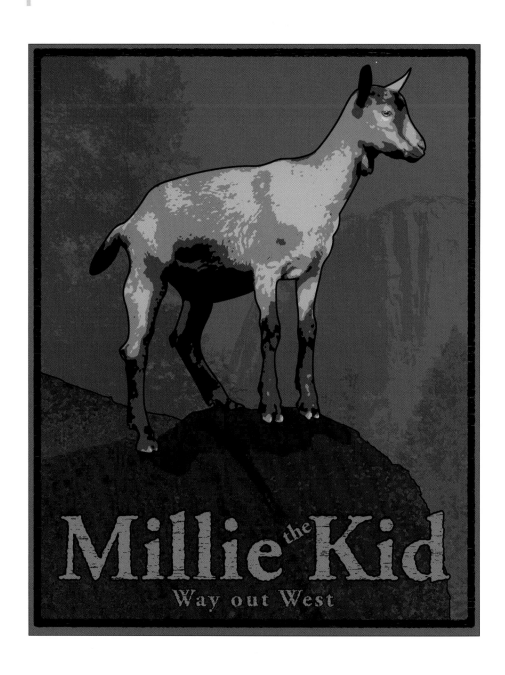

Create old-fashioned style graphics and type designs with this technique. First you design the basic graphic or typography in Illustrator. You can design it in Photoshop if you don't have Illustrator, but Illustrator is much easier to use for this part of the technique. Then you'll use Photoshop filters to roughen up the graphic and apply texture to it and its background. The results are flat, rough, and distressed. It's similar to old woodcut or stenciled graphics.

1   Create a graphic in Illustrator and save it. Open the file in Photoshop. Double-click the layer name in the Layers palette, and rename the layer Graphic.

If you want to create the artwork in Photoshop, use the pen tool, type tool, or shape tools; then choose Layer > Rasterize and select the appropriate layer type.

Rasterize the graphics or type

2   Option/Alt-click the New Layer button in the Layers palette. Name the new layer Background, and fill it with a color. Move the Graphic layer above the Background layer in the Layers palette.

3   Create a selection of the graphic by Command/Ctrl-clicking the thumbnail of the Graphic layer. Choose Select > Save Selection to create a new alpha channel. Name the new channel Graphic. Click OK.

Using Illustrator artwork in Photoshop

You can bring Illustrator files into Photoshop four different ways: using the Place, Export and Open, Copy and Paste, or the Open command. For precise instructions on how to do each technique, see Appendix B on page 318.

Shortcut: Selections

- Select All:
  Command/Ctrl+A
- Deselect:
  Command/Ctrl+D
- Reselect (the last selection):
  Shift+Command/Ctrl+D
- Select Inverse (of the
  current selection):
  Shift+Command/Ctrl+I

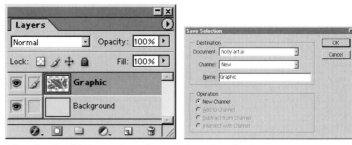

Move the Graphic layer above the Background layer

Save the selection

4 Display the Channels palette and click the name Graphic to view the Graphic channel. Choose Select > Deselect.

It's necessary to make a channel so that you can use some of the filters in the next steps. The filters give the most consistent results on black-and-white images.

View the Graphic channel

5 Choose Filter > Brush Strokes > Sprayed Strokes. Experiment with the values. The effect will vary depending on the file resolution and the size of the graphics. You want to roughen the edges just a bit in this step. Click OK.

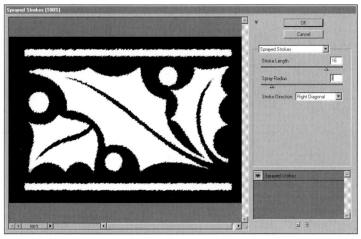

Apply the Sprayed Strokes filter

6 Choose Filter > Sketch > Stamp. Experiment with the values. As with the Sprayed Strokes filter, the effect will vary depending on the file resolution and the size of the graphics. This filter smooths out the edges. Click OK.

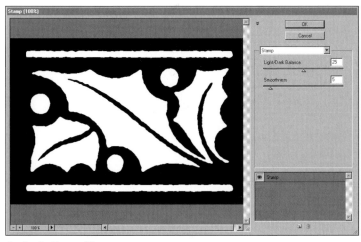

Apply the Stamp filter

Roughening edges on digital woodcuts

The balance between the Sprayed Strokes filter and the Stamp filter determines the amount of roughness added to the edges of the graphics. The result depends on the file resolution and the size of the graphic. Here are a few combinations to give you a head start on your tests.

Original graphic

Step 5: Stroke Length = 12, Spray Radius = 7

Step 5: Stroke Length = 1, Spray Radius = 7

Step 6: Light/Dark Balance = 15, Smoothness = 15

Shortcut: Load channel selections

Load a selection from the Channels palette without viewing the channel by Command/Ctrl-clicking the channel's thumbnail. In Windows, you can also Ctrl+right-click the thumbnail to load it as a selection.

This shortcut also works if you want to load a layer's pixels as a selection. Just Command/Ctrl-click the layer thumbnail.

7   Return to the Layers palette and click the Graphic layer to activate it. Option/Alt-click the New Layer button. Create a new layer named Rough Graphic. Turn off the Graphic layer.

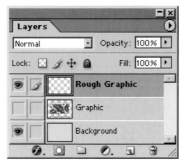

Create the Rough Graphic layer

8   Choose Select > Load Selection, and choose Graphic as the selection channel. Click OK.

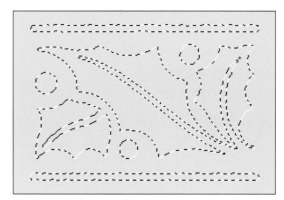

Load selection from the Graphic channel

9   Select a foreground color in the Color palette, and press Option+Delete/Alt+Backspace to fill the selection on the Rough Graphic layer. Deselect.

Fill selection with the foreground color

10 Press the D key to return the foreground and background colors to their default values. With the Rough Graphic layer selected in the Layers palette, click the Add Layer Mask button at the bottom of the palette.

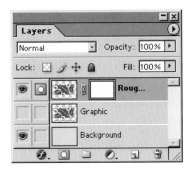

Create a layer mask

11 Choose Filter > Pixelate > Mezzotint. Select the Medium Strokes type, and click OK.

This filter adds texture to your graphic. If you want more texture, you can apply the filter more than once.

Shortcut: Hide and show a layer mask

To toggle a layer mask on and off in the Layers palette, Shift-click the layer mask thumbnail.

Apply the Mezzotint filter to the layer mask

12 Create a new layer and name it Extra Texture. Repeat steps 8 through 11. Set the layer blending mode to Multiply and adjust the layer opacity if desired. Click the Extra Texture layer mask and choose Image > Adjustments > Invert. This inversion allows just a small amount of texture to appear on the layer.

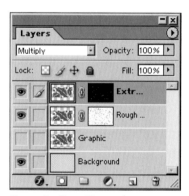

Create the Extra Texture layer

13 Create a new layer and name it Background Texture. Repeat steps 9 through 12. Move it just above the Background layer in the Layers palette.

Add texture to the Background layer

14 If you want to paint parts of your graphic different colors, click the Lock Transparent Pixels button in the Layers palette before you start painting. Don't forget to paint on both the Rough Graphic layer and the Extra Texture layer.

Recolor parts of the Graphic and Extra Texture layers

Section 3 | Type effects

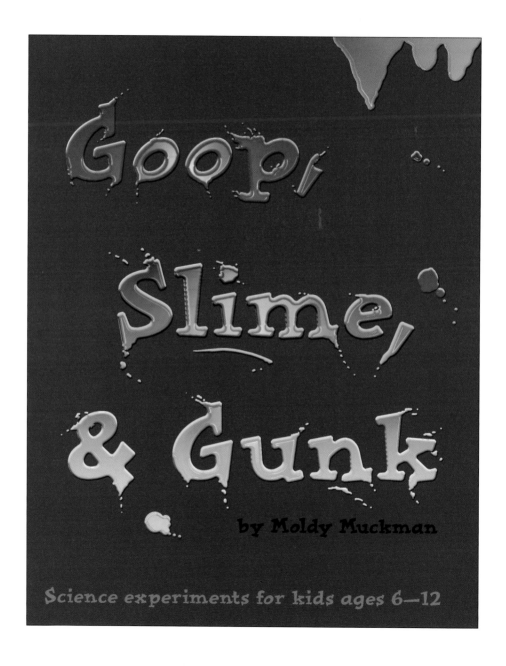

Making your headline or logo look like it's a puddle of readable paint is really easy with this technique. Choose a typeface that has an interesting design with swashes, swirls, and plenty of variation in the width of the strokes. Script typefaces tend to look the best. Use the Plaster filter to give the type dimension and lighting, and then colorize the type with an adjustment layer. The standard technique produces the type layer with its original transparency intact. If you want fatter type or eroded type, follow the variation instructions and merge the type with a background color.

Wet-paint type

1   Press the D key to set the foreground and background colors to their defaults of black and white. Create a new file and fill the Background layer with 100% black by pressing Option/Alt+Delete/Backspace.

2   Press the X key to switch white to the foreground color. Use the type tool to create the type that will become the wet paint type.

The best typefaces to use for this technique are script or calligraphic. If you want a slightly eroded look, choose a face with more pronounced thicks and thins.

Create white type

3   Choose Layer > Rasterize > Type to convert the editable type into pixels on a transparent background.

Rounding the edges of squared type designs

If you want to use the Wet-paint Type technique on a typeface that has squared corners, try using the Median filter to round it out before you begin.

1   Follow steps 1 through 3 of the Wet-paint Type technique.

2   Choose Filter > Noise > Median. Adjust the Radius until the edges and corners of the typeface are rounded. Click OK.

3   Continue with step 4 of the Wet-paint Type technique.

Creating a paint-drip brush

It's difficult to create paint drips that look randomly placed and sized. You can create a special brush for this purpose. Start with the following specifications and then change the values as needed to make the brush work with your art. This brush works best with a pressure-sensitive tablet, but one is not required.

1 Open the Brushes palette.
2 Select the Hard Round 19 pixel brush. Change the diameter to 87 pixels
3 Select Shape Dynamics and use these settings:
     Size Jitter = 81
     Control = Pen Pressure
     Angle Jitter = 11
     Roundness Jitter = 76
     Minimum Roundness = 47
4 Select Scattering and use these settings:
     Scattering = 196
     Control = Pen Pressure

Several strokes painted with the paint-drip brush

Paint drips with Plaster filter applied

To apply filters to type, you must first render type into pixels.

4   Use the brush tool to paint white drips and drops on the type layer.

Several brush sizes were combined to create the drips in this example. The brush strokes won't look much like drips at this point, but they will turn into small blobs of paint later.

Add paint drips to the type

5   Option/Alt-drag the type layer thumbnail onto the New Layer button at the bottom of the Layers palette. Name the new layer Wet Paint. The type layer will be used for a later step.

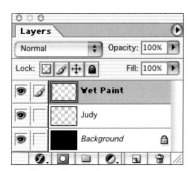

Duplicate the type layer

6   With the foreground color still set to white and the Wet Paint layer selected, choose Filter > Sketch > Plaster. Start with these values: Image Balance = 22, Smoothness = 2, and

Light = Top. Adjust the values until you are happy with the preview, and then click OK.

Apply the Plaster filter to the type and paint drips

7 Option/Alt-click the New Adjustment Layer button in the Layers palette. Choose Hue/Saturation as the type. Select the Use Previous Layer to Create Clipping Mask option in the New Layer dialog box so that the adjustment affects only the Wet Paint layer. Click OK to open the Hue/Saturation dialog box.

8 Select the Colorize option to apply color to the Wet Paint layer. Turn on the Preview option and adjust the Hue, Saturation, and Lightness sliders until you like the way the wet-paint type looks. Click OK.

Colorize applies color to the image while retaining the highlight, midtone, and shadow values.

Add an adjustment layer   *Set the Colorize option*

9 Evaluate the results with the current background. If you are satisfied, save the file. You can change the color by double-

Getting predictable color from the Plaster filter

The Plaster filter uses both the foreground and the background colors to create its effect. The original type color does not matter. The Plaster filter uses the foreground color to define the highlight areas and the background color to define the shadow areas. The Wet-Paint Type technique uses white and black to give you the most flexibility for changing and editing colors later. If you want to experiment with different effects, try starting with colors other than white and black.

Foreground and background colors selected

Plaster filter applied

clicking the Hue/Saturation adjustment thumbnail in the Layers palette and altering the Hue value.

Notice that the Plaster filter maintains the original transparency mask so that the type is no thicker or thinner than it was in step 4.

Colorized type

10 If you prefer a satiny finish to the paint surface instead of a shiny one, skip this step. To add a small, shiny highlight to the paint, select the Wet Paint layer and choose Filter > Artistic > Plastic Wrap. Start with these values and then adjust for your image: Highlight Strength = 20, Detail = 15, and Smoothness = 6.

Apply the Plastic Wrap filter to the type and paint drips

11 Click OK and save the file. Continue with the variations if you want fat or thin type, or if you want a different color highlight than white.

Completed type

Fat wet-paint type

1　Follow steps 1 through 5 of the Wet-paint Type technique.
Then duplicate the black Background layer by Option/Alt-
dragging the Background layer thumbnail onto the New
Layer button at the bottom of the Layers palette. Move the
duplicate layer up just beneath the Wet Paint layer.

2　Select the Wet Paint layer and choose Merge Down from the
Layers palette menu.

A solid layer is required here because the Plaster filter needs a
layer with no transparent pixels to be able to spread the type and
make it look fatter (or thinner).

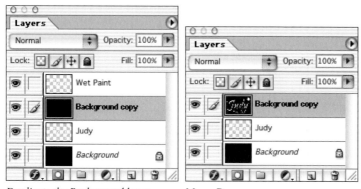

Duplicate the Background layer　　*Merge Down*

3 With the foreground color set to white and the Background Copy layer selected, choose Filter > Sketch > Plaster. Start with these values: Image Balance = 8 and Smoothness = 12. Adjust the values until you are happy with the preview, and then click OK.

To make the type even fatter, decrease the Image Balance or increase the Smoothness amount.

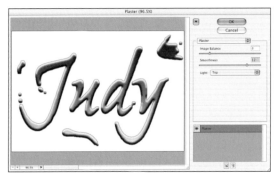

Apply the Plaster filter to the type and paint drips

4 Continue with steps 7 through 11 of the Wet-paint Type technique to complete the process.

The result will be a solid layer with white as the background. You can remove the white, if desired, by using the selection tools to select and delete the white. Be careful not to delete any white highlights that are within the letterforms.

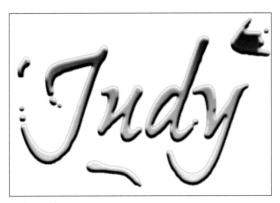

Colorize the type

Variation: Thin wet-paint type

For thinner or eroded-looking type, follow the Fat
Wet-paint Type technique, but use 46 for Image Balance and
6 for Smoothness with the Plaster filter.

Thin wet-paint type

Colored wet-paint highlight or shadow

To make the wet-paint type look more interesting and realistic,
you may want to change the color of the highlight or shadow. If
so, follow these steps. For shadows, adjust the highlight sliders
in step 4.

1   Create some wet-paint type using the Wet-paint Type
    technique. In the Layers palette, select the Hue/Saturation
    layer and choose Merge Down from the Layers palette
    menu.

2   In the Layers palette, double-click the name of the original
    type layer that you created in step 4 of the Wet-paint Type
    technique. Change the name to Highlight. Set the blending
    mode to Multiply and turn on the Lock Transparent Pixels
    option. Move the Highlight layer directly above the Wet
    Paint layer.

Locking transparent pixels

Type layers have transparent pixels locked by default. But once the type layer is rasterized, the transparent pixels are no longer locked. Unlocked transparency is great if you want to paint on the layer. But what if you want to change the color of everything on the layer while retaining the soft edges of the type and brush strokes? Turn on the Lock Transparent Pixels option in the Layers palette. With transparency locked, any semitransparent pixels will retain their transparency and simply change color. Any completely transparent pixels will not change.

Transparent pixels locked

Original image

Filled type retains anti-aliased edges

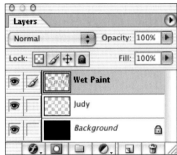

Merge Down

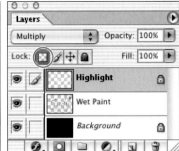

Change the type layer settings and name

3 With the Highlight layer still selected, choose a color that you want to be the highlight color from the Color palette. Fill the Highlight layer with the color by pressing Option/Alt+Delete/Backspace.

Because you locked the transparent pixels in step 2, only the areas containing the type and the paint drips will be filled with the color. Also, because the blending mode is set to Multiply, the fill will not look like a flat color. Next, you will adjust the shadow and midtone areas so that the highlight color only shows up in the lightest areas.

Fill the Highlight layer with solid color

4 Double-click the Highlight layer thumbnail to open the Layer Style dialog box. Option/Alt-click and drag the shadows control for the This Layer slider. Start with the settings shown below and then adjust for your image. (For a shadow color, move the highlight sliders to the left.)

Option/Alt-clicking lets you split the slider and make a finer and smoother transition between values.

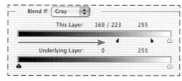

Adjust layer blending

5   Click OK. Try setting the Highlight layer mode to Color Burn, Soft Light, or Darken for a different look.

Highlight layer set to Multiply

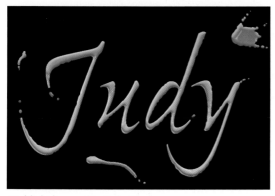

Highlight layer set to Color Burn

Corroded type

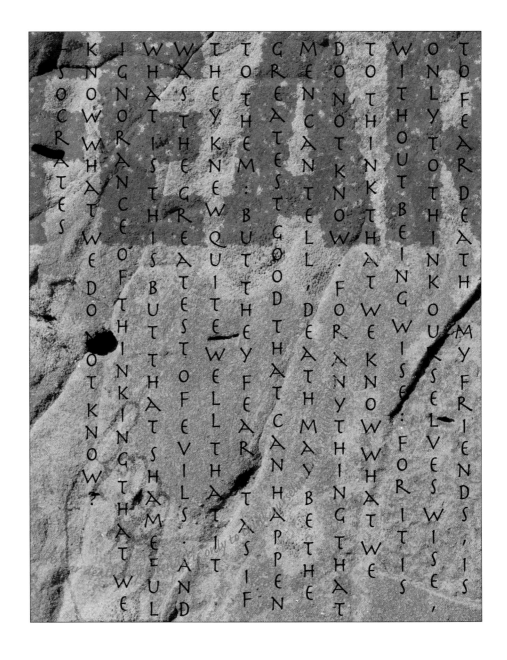

Some designers try to simulate an eroded or weathered type effect by making a series of photocopies in which each copy is made from the previous copy. The following technique lets you achieve a similar look with more control and less wasted paper. The basic technique produces a typeface with holes in it and corroded edges. The variation gives you a sketchy, scratchy look. A serif typeface design such as Times or Caslon will work well with the Eroded Type technique if you want the thin parts of the letters to look eaten away.

Corroded type

1   Create or open the file to which you want to add the corroded type.

Create or open a new file

2   Choose New Channel from the Channels palette menu. Select the Selected Areas option and name the channel Type. Click OK.

Channels are always grayscale, and they usually look like film negatives. In this technique, the channel looks like a positive grayscale image, and the areas of black and gray are the selection areas.

Changing channel thumbnail sizes

When working with type or other intricate selections in a channel, it can be difficult to read the thumbnail in the Channels palette. Being able to read the thumbnail is especially important if you have several versions of the same graphic in different channels. To change the size of the thumbnails, choose Palette Options from the Channel palette menu. Then select the thumbnail size that fits your needs.

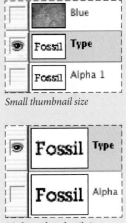

Small thumbnail size

Medium thumbnail size

Kerning or tracking

Depending on the typeface and the letter combinations you use, you may need to adjust the tracking or kerning between the letters. Before you do this, try selecting the type layer in the Layers palette. In the Character palette, choose either Optical or Metrics from the kerning pop-up menu. These options will adjust letterspacing depending on which font you use.

If you want to kern between two characters, select the type tool and click between the characters. Then enter a value for the Kerning amount. If you want to add or remove space for an entire selection or type layer, select the type and enter a value for the Tracking amount.

Kerning adjusts the space between character pairs. Depending on the font, it can be different amounts for different pairs. For example, an uppercase *T* followed by a lowercase *e* would need a different amount of space between them than an uppercase *T* and an uppercase *H*. Tracking adds the same amount of space between all selected characters.

Set the kerning between two characters

Set the tracking between selected characters

Create a new channel

3 Press the D key to return the foreground and background colors to white and black. Then press the X key to reverse their positions. Use the type tool to create black type in the Type channel; then press Return/Enter. Use the move tool to position the type while it is selected.

Type created in channels becomes a selection, not an editable type layer.

Create type in the channel

4 While the type is still selected, choose Filter > Pixelate > Mezzotint. Choose Grainy Dots for the Type of mezzotint. Click OK.

The preview may show the mezzotint affecting the white area as well as the type. But as long as the type is selected, the filter will apply only to the selected area.

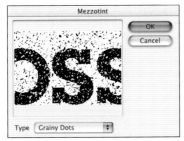

Use the Mezzotint filter on the type selection

5 Deselect the type and choose Filter > Brush Strokes > Spatter. Use the preview to determine the values to use for Spray Radius and Smoothness. The amount will vary depending on the typeface, type size, and personal preference.

Apply the Spatter filter

6 If you want to smooth out the holes a bit, choose Filter > Noise > Median. Turn on the Preview option, and select a Radius amount based on how smooth and rounded you want the type to be. Then click OK.

Shortcut: Load selections

Load a selection quickly from any channel by simply Command/Ctrl-clicking the channel thumbnail in the Channels palette. The channel doesn't have to be visible to do this.

To load the transparency mask of any layer, Command/Ctrl-click the layer thumbnail in the Layers palette. Using this shortcut with type layers is very handy because they are created with transparent backgrounds; the effect is the same as using a type mask tool.

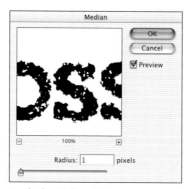

Apply the Median filter

7 Save the file. The Type channel is now complete and ready to be used as a selection.

You'll use this selection in the next step to create the colored, corroded type.

Type channel is ready to use

8 To add a color type layer to your artwork, open the Layers palette. Click the Background layer to view the composite color image again. Create a new layer and name it Corroded Type.

9 With the Corroded Type layer still selected, choose Select > Load Selection and load the Type channel as the selection.

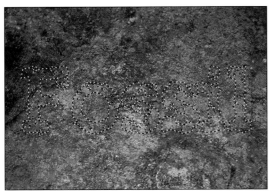

Load the Type channel as a selection

Shortcut: Fill a selection

To fill a layer or selection with the foreground color, choose a color in the Color palette, and then press Option/Alt+Delete/Backspace. To fill with the background color, press Command/Ctrl+Delete/Backspace.

10 Select a foreground color as a fill for the type. Choose Edit > Fill and fill the selection with the foreground color. Save the file.

You can change the color later without reloading the Type channel selection. Just turn on the Lock Transparent Pixels option in the Layers palette for the Corroded Type layer, and fill. Only nontransparent areas will fill with color.

Fill the selection with color

Paint Daubs filter

Torn Edges filter

Sprayed Strokes filter

Glass filter

Eroded type

1   Choose a typeface design that has varied thickness in the letterforms. Follow the Corroded Type technique, except replace steps 4 through 6 with the following: Deselect the type. Choose Filter > Artistic > Palette Knife. Adjust the Softness, Stroke Size, and Stroke Detail until you have the desired amount of erosion. Don't click OK.

Apply the Palette Knife filter

2   Click the Add New Effect button at the bottom of the Filter Gallery dialog box. Choose Torn Edges from the pop-up menu. Start with these values: Image Balance = 25, Smoothness = 11, Contrast = 17, and then adjust them for your typeface and size. Click OK.

Apply the Torn Edges filter

3   Continue with steps 7 through 10 of the Corroded Type technique to complete the effect.

Eroded type

Variation: Exaggerated corroded type

Follow the Corroded Type technique, except replace steps 4 through 6 with the following:

1   Deselect. Choose Filter > Brush Strokes > Sprayed Strokes. Use a Vertical Stroke Direction and start with a Stroke Length of 12 and a Spray Radius of 15. Adjust these values to your taste.

2   For a really corroded look, reapply the filter with the same settings.

Corroded type variation

Chrome type can be created in Photoshop several ways, and most are fairly involved. You can do this technique in two stages. The Shiny Chrome Type technique shows you how to create embossed type that looks shiny and metallic, for a gray type effect that can be colorized quickly with a Hue/Saturation adjustment layer. If you want to create the effect of the sky or another image reflecting off the type, continue with the Type with a Sky Reflection technique. Create your own sky using the Clouds filter or bring in another file with a sky for a different effect.

Shiny chrome type

1   Create a new RGB file, and use the type tool to create the type that will become "chrome."

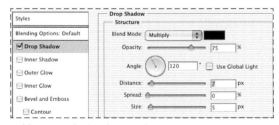

Marti
Tools

Create the type

2   Click the Add Layer Style button in the Layers palette, and choose Drop Shadow to give the type some dimension. Turn on the Preview option, and adjust the values for your type style and size. Don't click OK yet.

Add a Drop Shadow layer style

Shortcut: Change type sizes quickly

Change the point size of selected type quickly with the keyboard. You must first select the type tool. The shortcut won't work if you just click the type layer in the Layers palette.

- Increase the point size by 2 points: Command/Ctrl+ >

- Decrease the point size by 2 points: Command/Ctrl+ <

- Increase the point size by 10 points: Command/Ctrl+ Option/Alt+ >

- Decrease the point size by 10 points: Command/Ctrl+ Option/Alt+ <

Feathering selections

Adding feathering to an existing selection will soften the edge of the selection. You can add feathering to an existing selection or you can specify a feathering amount for the selection tools. The feathering effect depends on the size of the selection and its resolution. Higher resolutions may require a higher feathering amount.

No feathering (300 pixels per inch)

3 pixels feathering (300 ppi)

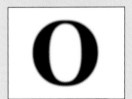

6 pixels feathering (300 ppi)

12 pixels feathering (300 ppi)

3 In the Styles list, click Color Overlay to select the style and open its options. Click the color swatch and change the color to this mix: R = 161, G = 171, and B = 219. Click OK in the color picker. Don't click OK yet in the Layer Style dialog box.

Add a blue Color Overlay layer style

4 In the Styles list, click Inner Shadow to select the style and open its options. Use the following settings: Blend Mode = Multiply, Opacity = 75%, Color = Black, Angle = 120°, Distance = 4 px, Choke = 0%, and Size = 6 px. Don't click OK yet.

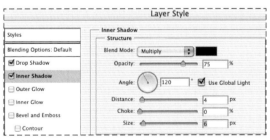

Add an Inner Shadow layer style

5 In the Styles list, click Inner Shadow to select the style and open its options. Use the following settings:

Blend Mode = Multiply, Opacity = 75%, Color = Black, Angle = 120°, Distance = 4 px, Choke = 0%, and Size = 6 px. Don't click OK yet.

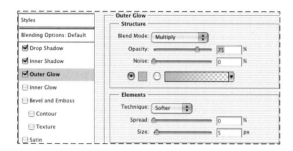

Add a blue Outer Glow layer style

6   In the Styles list, click Inner Glow to select the style and open its options. Use the following settings: Blend Mode = Multiply, Opacity = 40%, Color = Black, Technique = Softer, Source = Center, and Size = 27. Click the arrow next to the contour thumbnail to open the Contour pop-up palette. Then click the arrow to the right to open the pop-up palette menu and choose Small List to display the contours by name. Select the Ring contour. Click outside of the pop-up palette to close it. Don't click OK yet.

7   In the Styles list, click Bevel and Emboss to select the style and open its options. Use the following settings: Style = Inner Bevel, Technique = Smooth, Depth = 131%, Direction = Up, Size = 7 px, Soften = 0 px, Angle = 120°, and

Changing the grid in the Contour Editor dialog box

If you have several points to plot on the Contour grid, a finer grid cam be helpful. To toggle between the default grid and the finer grid, Option/Alt-click in the grid area. The grid remains as you last used it until you reuse it. This technique can also be used with the Curves grid.

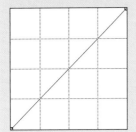

Default grid size

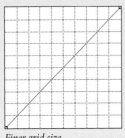

Finer grid size

Altitude = 30°. Gloss Contour = Ring (click the arrow button to display the palette menu); Highlight Mode = Screen, Color = White, and Opacity = 100%; Shadow Mode = Overlay, Color = Black, and Opacity = 75%.
Don't click OK yet.

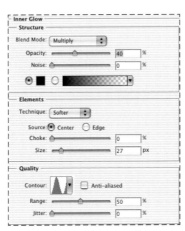

Add an Inner Glow layer style

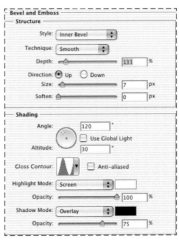

Add a Bevel and Emboss layer style

Type with six layer styles including Inner Glow and Bevel and Emboss

8 In the Styles list, click Satin to select the style and open its options. Use the following settings: Blend Mode = Screen, Color = White, Opacity = 78%, Angle = 137°, Distance = 14 px, Size = 16 px, and choose both the Anti-aliased and Invert options. Click the arrow next to the contour

thumbnail to open the Contour pop-up palette. Then click the arrow to the right to display the pop-up palette menu and choose Contours from the bottom of the menu. When the warning dialog box appears, click Append. Select the Sawtooth 2 contour. Click outside of the pop-up palette to close it. Don't click OK yet.

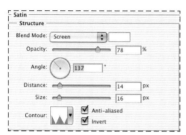

Add a Satin layer style

Shortcut: Move points in the Contour Editor or Curves dialog box

Click the Contour grid to add a new point or select a point already plotted on the curve. While the point is still selected, press one of the arrow keys to move the point by 1 unit (2 units in the Curves dialog box). To move it by 6 units (15 units in the Curves dialog box), hold down the Shift key while pressing one of the arrow keys.

9 In the Styles list, click the Contour option (it appears just beneath Bevel and Emboss) to display its options. Click the contour thumbnail to open the Contour Editor. Move the left point on the grid to these coordinates: Input = 0% and Output = 64%. The right point's coordinates should be Input = 100% and Output = 100%. Click OK to close the Contour Editor dialog box; then click OK to close the Layer Style dialog box. Save the file, and stop here if you are satisfied with blue-gray chrome type. To create a distorted reflection, continue with the next technique, "Type with a sky reflection" on page 168.

If you want to color the type before stopping here, add a Hue/Saturation adjustment layer, select the Colorize option, and adjust the hue and saturation until the type is the preferred color and brightness.

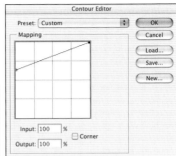

Add a contour to the Bevel and Emboss layer style

Edit the contour

How resolution affects blurring

When following the techniques in this book, keep in mind that the resolution of your file is critical when using filters or functions that involve entering pixel amounts. For example, notice how different the files below look after the same amount of Gaussian blur was applied. Each image was blurred by 3 pixels. The images in this book are all 300 pixels per inch (ppi). If your resolution differs, you may need to change the amount you use when entering pixel values.

72 ppi

150 ppi

300 ppi

Completed blue-gray chrome type

Type with a sky reflection

1   Complete the "Shiny chrome type" technique on page 163. Then Command/Ctrl-click the type thumbnail in the Layers palette to load its outlines as a selection.

2   Choose Window > Channels to display the Channels palette. Option/Alt-click the Save Selection as Channel button at the bottom of the Channels palette to save the selection. Name it Blurred Type. Click OK.

3   In the Channels palette, select the Blurred Type channel that you just created.

4   Deselect (Command/Ctrl+D). Choose Filter > Blur > Gaussian Blur. Blur the type quite a bit, using this example

as a guide. Your Radius amount will vary depending on the file resolution and type size. Click OK.

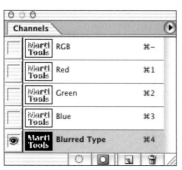

Create the Blurred Type channel   *Use Gaussian Blur to blur the channel*

Shortcut: View different channels

You can view different channels without using the Channels palette. Simply press Command/Ctrl+ 1 through 9 to view the different alpha channels. Command/Ctrl+ ~ (tilde sign) displays the composite channel.

Press Command/Ctrl plus:
~ = RGB composite
1 = Red channel
2 = Green channel
3 = Blue channel
4 – 9 = Alpha channels
\ = Layer mask of selected
    layer

5 Choose Duplicate Channel from the Channels palette menu. In the Duplicate As text box, name the channel Blurred Type Map; for Destination, choose New as the Document. Click OK. Save the Blurred Type Map file, noting where you saved it, and close the file.

6 If you prefer to use a different image for the reflection, drag it into the file and skip steps 7 through 9.

7 Click any layer in the Layers palette to reactivate the composite view of the type file. Option/Alt-click the New Layer button and name the new layer Sky. Move the Sky layer to the top of the layer stack.

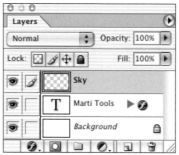

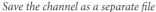

Save the channel as a separate file   *Create the Sky layer*

Creating your own clouds

The Clouds filters use the foreground and background colors to generate a sky and cloud image. If you want contrasty clouds, hold down Option/Alt when using or reusing the Clouds filter. Each application of the filter completely replaces the image, so keep applying the filter until you like the result. Press Command/Ctrl+F to reapply the filter.

To experiment with unusual color and texture mixtures, try Difference Clouds. Reapplying this filter has a cumulative effect.

Filter > Render > Clouds

Filter > Render > Clouds while depressing Option/Alt

Filter > Render > Difference Clouds with magenta and gold colors selected

8 Choose RGB Sliders from the Color palette menu. Select white as the background color and blue as the foreground color, with the following mix or adjusted to your own taste: R = 154, G = 176, and B = 218.

9 With the Sky layer selected in the Layers palette, choose Filter > Render > Clouds. To get more contrasting clouds, hold down Option/Alt as you choose the Clouds filter. Repeat this step until you have a cloudy sky that you like.

Each time you run the Clouds filter, the results will change.

Use the Clouds filter to create a sky image

10 Choose Filter > Distort > Glass. Click the arrow button to the right of the Texture menu and choose Load Texture. Navigate to the Blurred Type Map file that you saved in step 5 and click Load. Use a Distortion of 20 and a Smoothness of 4. Click OK.

Apply the Glass filter

11 Command/Ctrl-click the type thumbnail in the Layers palette to load its outlines as a selection. Select the Sky layer in the Layers palette and click the Add Layer Mask button at the bottom of the Layers palette. Set the layer mode to Linear Burn.

12 Double-click the Sky layer thumbnail in the Layers palette to open the Layer Style dialog box. Option/Alt-click the highlights control for the Underlying Layer to split the control; then drag each half of the control until some of the highlights appear and you like the effect. Click OK.

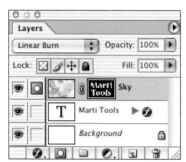

Add a layer mask to the Sky layer

Adjust the layer blending

13 Save the file. If you want to change the type face or size at any time, the type will still maintain its chrome effect.

Completed reflected sky type

Embossing type is extremely easy and flexible with the Layer Style feature in Photoshop. The first technique applies an embossed effect to type with the same color as the Background layer to make the type look as if it's really embossed on the background texture. Once you've embossed your type, you can give it the look and feel of gold metal with the second technique.

Embossed type

1   Open or create a file that will be the background surface for the embossed type. For best results, use a surface that contains texture. Select white as your foreground color. Select the type tool and enter your text.

Create white type on a textured surface

2   With the type layer selected, click the Add Layer Style button at the bottom of the Layers palette. Use the pop-up menu to choose Bevel and Emboss, and in the Layer Style dialog box, set the style to Inner Bevel. Don't click OK yet.

Don't worry about the other settings too much at this point. You may want to go back and adjust them at the end of the technique.

3   Click Blending Options in the Styles list on the left side of the Layer Style dialog box. In the Advanced Blending section, set the Fill Opacity to 10%.

Got texture?

Create a surface for your embossed type quickly with a couple of different filters. Here are three ideas:
- Choose Filter > Texture > Texturizer. Choose a default texture from the Textures pop-up menu or click the button to its right to load a new texture. Photoshop will open the Textures folder in the Presets folder. Try using Rust Flakes or Stucco.
- Try using the Fibers filter for a wood grain effect. First select a foreground and background color, which the Fibers filter uses to create a texture. Then choose Filter > Render > Fibers.
- Choose Filter > Sketch > Note Paper. Play with the settings until you find a texture you like.

For more ideas and recipes for textures, see "Stone and Stucco Textures" on page 72, or "Wood-grain Textures" on page 84.

Copying a layer style to another layer

Once you've perfected a layer style, you may want to use it on another layer or in another file. To copy a layer style, simply click the layer in the Layers palette that contains the style you want to duplicate. Choose Layer > Layer Style > Copy Layer Style. Then click the layer you want to stylize in the Layers palette and choose Layer > Layer Style > Paste Layer Style to apply the copied layer style.

Leaving just 10% white makes the type pop off the background a bit. You may want to adjust this percentage depending on the background.

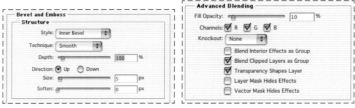

Set the Inner Bevel style   *Set the Fill Opacity*

4   Click OK to view the results.

If the effect is too subtle, double-click the effects ("*f*") icon on the type layer to reopen the Layer Style dialog box, and adjust the Fill Opacity. You can also exaggerate the effect by clicking Bevel and Emboss on the left side of the dialog box to redisplay the style's Structure options. Then increase the size or depth of the embossing.

Final embossed type

Metallic-gold embossed type

1   Create a file that will be the background surface for the gold type. For the most dramatic results, use a dark background. Create a gold foreground color of R = 249, G = 215, and B = 121. Select the type tool and enter your text.

Create gold type on a dark surface

2   Command/Ctrl-click the type layer thumbnail in the Layers palette to create a selection of its transparency mask.

Create a selection of the type's transparency mask

3   Choose Select > Save Selection to save the selection to a new alpha channel. Name the channel Type Mask.

4   Deselect. Click the Type Mask channel in the Channels palette. Choose Filter > Blur > Gaussian Blur to soften the image.

This channel will be used in step 8 as a mask. More blur will produce a rounder, less beveled effect. Less blur will produce more defined bevels. This example used a 3-pixel radius.

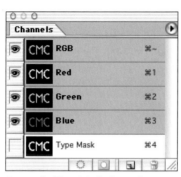

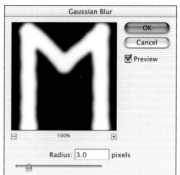

Create the Type Mask channel   *Blur the Type Mask channel*

5 Reselect the type layer in the Layers palette, click the Add
Layer Style button, and choose Bevel and Emboss from the
pop-up menu. Set the style to Inner Bevel and leave the
settings at their default values.

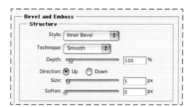

Set the Inner Bevel style

6 Make any final copy changes to your type layer. You'll apply
a lighting effect that rasterizes the type and renders it no
longer editable with the type tools.

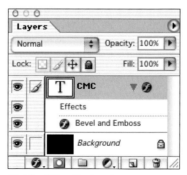

Finish editing the type layer

7 Choose Filter > Render > Lighting Effects. At the alert, click OK.

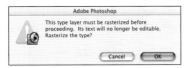

Click OK to rasterize the type layer

8 Select 2 O'clock Spotlight as the Style. Choose Type Mask as the Texture Channel. Deselect the White is High option to avoid making the type look debossed.

Lighting Effects comes with a set of predefined lighting styles that you may want to try. Use 2 O'clock Spotlight to replicate the results shown here.

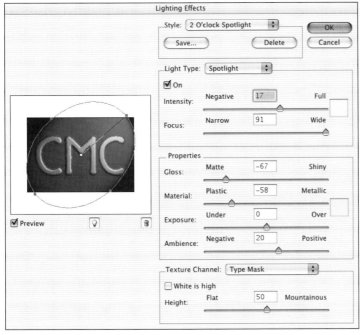

Use the 2 O'clock Spotlight style with the Type Mask as the Texture Channel

9 With the type layer still active, choose Filter > Artistic > Plastic Wrap. Use the following values: Highlight Strength = 15, Detail = 9, and Smoothness = 7. Click OK.

Scaling type the professional way

If you must scale type, do it by changing the point size with the type tool, the Character palette or the tool options bar. Avoid using the transformation commands with type. Using the Character palette, to scale your type will ensure that the letterforms retain their predesigned spacing and kerning. Also, it ensures that you won't accidentally distort the letterforms when scaling, which can happen if you use the transformation commands. If a typeface is too fat to fit, choose a thinner one. Don't distort the typeface. It makes the type look badly designed—a telltale sign of an amateur designer.

Altering a filter result

To change or lessen the effect of a filter or an image adjustment effect, use Edit > Fade immediately after you've applied the effect. The Fade command is only available just after the filter or adjustment is applied, and otherwise is grayed out. Use it to reduce the effect by lowering the opacity. A lower opacity effectively lessens the amount that the filter or image adjustment is applied to the image. You can also change the look of the filter or image adjustment by choosing a different blend mode.

The Plastic Wrap filter will add more highlights to make the type appear more metallic.

10 Choose Edit > Fade Plastic Wrap. Set the mode to Hard Light to magnify the color, and click OK.

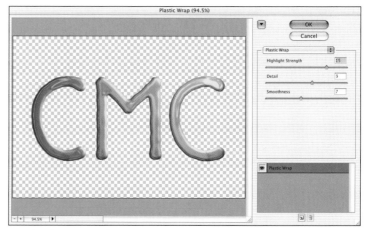

Use the Plastic Wrap filter

Set the Fade mode to Hard Light

11 Evaluate the results. If you want to adjust the color of the type, continue with the variation. If you are satisfied with the results, save the file.

Completed metallic-embossed type

Variation: color overlay

If you want to change the type color without altering the metallic effect, try the following variation.

1   Follow the Metallic-gold Embossed Type technique. Double-click the effects icon at the right of the type layer name in the Layers palette. This opens the Layer Style dialog box.

2   Click the words Color Overlay in the Styles list on the left side of the dialog box. Set the Mode to Hue and click the color swatch to open the color picker.

3   Select a color in the color picker. Turn on the Preview option to see the results. Click OK when you have the color you like.

Add a color overlay to colorize the type

Saving a layer style as a preset style

Here's how to save a layer style as a preset style.

1   Click the layer in the Layers palette that contains the style.

2   Do one of the following things:
   • Double-click the layer thumbnail to open the Layer Style dialog box; then click the New Style button.
   • Click in an empty area of the Styles palette.
   • Option/Alt-click the New Item button at the bottom of the Styles palette.
   • Choose New Style from the Styles palette menu.
   • Drag the selected layer onto the Styles palette or the New Item button at the bottom of the Styles palette.

3   Name the style and, if applicable, select Include Layer Blending Options. (This will include any General or Advanced blending options.) Click OK.

You can add outlines to type in Photoshop a couple of different ways. But the most flexible way is to add a stroke as a layer effect. The nice thing about using this method is that you can go back and change the thickness or color at any time. Here's how to make multiple, distinct color outlines around your type with a Stroke layer effect.

1   In a new or existing file, use the type tool to create the type that you want to outline. Typically, substantial sans serif typefaces work best, so experiment with different typefaces. Try to avoid very fine or light typefaces, because the outlines can sometimes overwhelm the original type design and make it illegible.

Create a type layer

2   Display the Character palette (Command/Ctrl+T), and adjust the tracking for the type layer. Make plenty of space between the letters so that the outlines don't touch. The more outlines you want, the more tracking you need to add. The following example used a tracking amount of 50.

3   In the Layers palette, click the Add Layer Style button and choose Stroke from the pop-up menu. Select a size for the stroke and choose Outside for Position. Set the Fill Type to Color and click the color swatch to select a color for the stroke. Move the Layer Style dialog box away from the type so that you can see the image. Click OK when you are happy with the effect.

Using just type outlines

You can create multiple outlines around your type and then remove the solid color from the shape of the letters, leaving behind only the outlines. Follow the steps for the Outlined Type technique. Then, in the Layers palette, select each type layer and set its Fill to 0%. The type won't be completely invisible until you adjust each layer's fill. (Adjusting the Fill percentage affects the pixels on the layer but not the layer effects.)

Original type with outlines

Set the Fill to 0% for each type layer

Type is invisible but the outlines still display

Creating multiple outlines with blend modes

To get an interesting but somewhat upredictable outline effect, follow the Outlined Type technique, but in step 3 for the Stroke effect, choose a blending mode other than Normal for the Stroke effects.

The following examples show the Multiply blending mode used for all three layers. Notice how the colors change with each added stroke. The results you get will depend on the modes and colors used.

One stroke added with Multiply mode

Second stroke added with Multiply mode

Third stroke added with Multiply mode

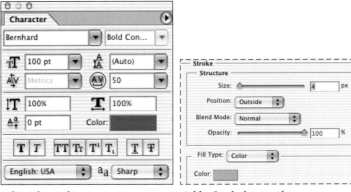

Adjust the tracking　　　*Add a Stroke layer style*

4　Evaluate the effect. If you want only one outline, save the file. If you want to add more outlines to the type, continue with step 5.

Type with one outline

5　To create the second outline, duplicate the type layer by dragging it onto the New Layer button at the bottom of the Layers palette. Rename the layer after the second stroke you will create. Drag the duplicate layer down below the original type layer in the Layers palette.

6 Double-click the Stroke effects (*f*) icon under the duplicated type layer to open the Layer Style dialog box. Change the color by clicking the color swatch. Increase the stroke size until you are happy with the effect, and then click OK.

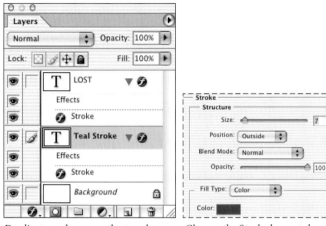

Duplicate and rename the type layer

Change the Stroke layer style

7 Repeat steps 5 and 6 for as many outlines as you want. Save the file.

Type with three outlines

Stroking type with a gradient

If you want the colors that outline your type to blend smoothly from one to another, stroke the type with a gradient. Follow the Outlined Type technique, but in step 3 for Fill Type, choose Gradient. Select a gradient by clicking the gradient swatch. Set the Style to Shape Burst.

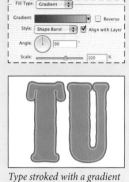

Type stroked with a gradient

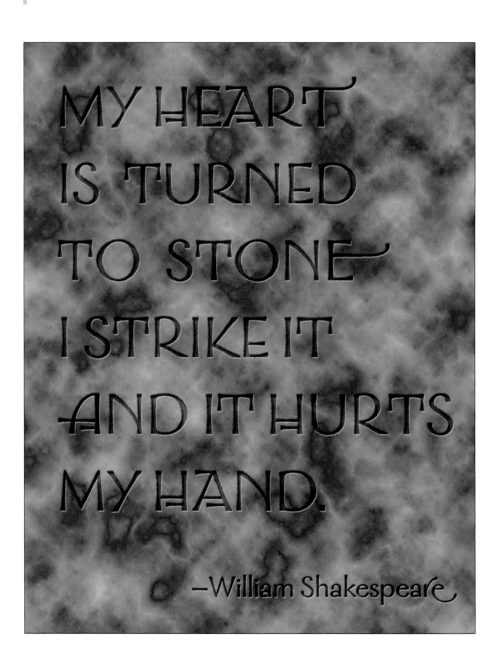

This technique makes your type look as if it were engraved into a surface. You can achieve a quick cutout effect by creating an Inner Shadow layer style for your type. But to make type really look carved from the surface texture, you'll need to add two more layer styles. One style creates the beveled edge of the type cut out of the surface, and one style adds the surface texture back into the type recess. This technique works well with a variety of different typefaces, but try to stay away from styles with very thin stems. Such fonts tend to fill in with shadow and don't look as good as those with a more evenly distributed thickness.

Shortcut: Reset default colors

Press the D key to return the foreground and background colors to black and white respectively. Press the X key to switch the colors.

1   Open a file with a texture or background surface image from which you will digitally carve type. Rename this layer Outer Texture.

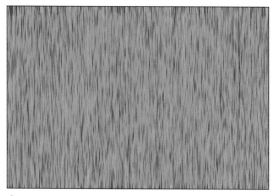

Open a texture image

2   Change the foreground color to white and create the text.

If the background color is currently white, press the X key to switch the foreground and background colors.

Shortcut: Move shadows manually

Not sure how many pixels or what angle to use for the shadow position? With the Layer Style dialog box open, move your pointer onto the image and notice that it changes to the move tool pointer. Click and begin to drag around on the image. You can position shadows this way instead of entering values in the dialog box. This shortcut works for both the Drop Shadow and Inner Shadow styles.

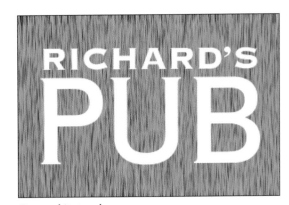

Create white type layer

3   Click the Add Layer Style button in the Layers palette, and choose Inner Shadow to add a cutout effect to the type layer. Turn on the Preview option, and adjust the values for your particular type style and letter combination. Don't click OK yet.

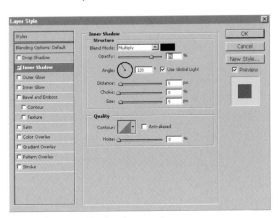

Create the Inner Shadow layer style

4   In the Styles list, click Inner Glow to select the style and open its options. Click the color swatch and change the glow color to black. Change the Blend Mode to Multiply, and set the Opacity to 10%. Choose Center for the Source. With the Preview option turned on, adjust the Opacity level until the letterform is light gray and has a slight inner shadow. Click OK.

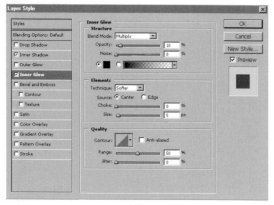

Add Inner Glow as a second layer style

5 Use the move tool to adjust the position of the type against the background. The type will remain editable. However, you'll make a layer mask from a selection of the type in step 7; after that, you won't be able to move the type.

Place the type in its final position

6 If you don't want the texture to show through the type, skip this step. Duplicate the texture layer, and name it Inner Texture. Move it beneath the Outer Texture layer.

About the Background layer

The Background layer is always the bottommost layer in a file—you can't move it up or down in the stack. You also can't change its blending mode or opacity. However, you can convert the Background layer to a regular layer. To do this, double-click the Background layer in the Layers palette. In the New Layer dialog box, name the layer and click OK.

To turn any layer into a Background layer, first make sure that the image doesn't already have a Background layer. Then choose Layer > New > Background from Layer.

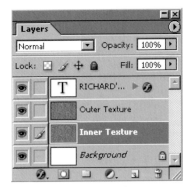

Create the Inner Texture layer

7 Command/Ctrl-click the type layer thumbnail to load a selection of its transparency mask. Choose Select > Inverse to select the transparent pixels on the type layer.

Select the inverse of the type layer transparency

8 Click the Outer Texture layer in the Layers palette and then click the Layer Mask button to create a mask.

Adding a layer mask creates edges of carved wood. In the next step, you'll add a layer style to bevel and highlight these edges.

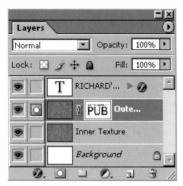

Create a layer mask on the Outer Texture layer

Copying and pasting a layer style

Once you've created a layer style, you can apply it to other layers without recreating it each time.
1   Select the layer in the Layers palette that contains the layer style.
2   Choose Layer > Layer Style > Copy Layer Style.
3   Select the layer in the Layers palette to which you will apply the style.
4   Choose Layer > Layer Style > Paste Layer Style.

9   With the Outer Texture layer still active, click the Add Layer Style button in the Layers palette, and choose Bevel and Emboss. Select Inner Bevel as the Style. Turn on the Preview option and adjust the values for your type style and letter combination.

You'll see the edges of the texture grow in depth. This example used a yellow highlight instead of white for a softer effect.

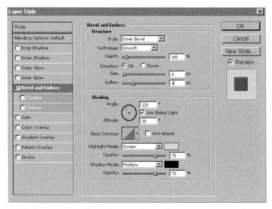

Add the Bevel and Emboss style to the Outer Texture layer

10   Evaluate the result. Adjust the layer style settings on the type or texture layer as desired. Some type styles and sizes need more adjustment than others. Once you are satisfied with the effect, click OK.

Opacity versus Fill opacity

When using layer styles, layer opacity and Fill opacity have different results. These settings appear in the upper right corner of the Layers palette (and in the Layer Style dialog box).Changing the opacity of a layer changes both the layer contents and its layer style. Changing the Fill opacity of a layer changes only the opacity of the layer contents; the layer style remains unchanged.

100% opacity, 100% Fill opacity

100% opacity, 30% Fill opacity

30% opacity, 100% Fill opacity

Adjust the layer style settings

11 Select the type layer, and change its blending mode to Multiply to reveal the texture on the Inner Texture layer.

12 If you are satisfied with the effect, save the file. If desired, you can adjust the layer styles to change the size of the shadows, bevels, or highlights.

Set the type layer blending mode to Multiply

Variation: Flat-color type

For a flat color inside the type, follow the Recessed Type technique. Then choose a new foreground color. Select the type layer and press Option/Alt+Delete/Backspace to fill the type with the new foreground color. Set the type layer mode to Normal.

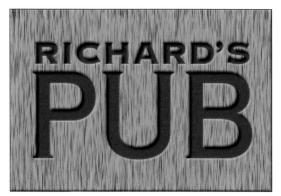

Create flat-colored type instead of white

Variation: Colored-texture type

For a colored texture inside the type, follow the Recessed Type technique. Then select the Inner Texture layer. Create a Hue/Saturation adjustment layer and group it with the Inner Texture layer. Change the Hue, Saturation, and Lightness for the effect you want.

This example used values of Hue = −180, Saturation = −71, and Lightness = −22.

Adjust the color on the Inner Texture layer

Scaling layer effects

It's great to use layer style presets or copy layer styles, but they may have been designed for a specific graphic or resolution. If you want to use the preset or copied layer style on other graphics at other resolutions, you must be able to scale it. For example, the following illustration shows a layer effect applied that was originally designed for a larger type size. The bottom illustration shows the layer style scaled down.

To scale a layer style, select the layer that has a layer style applied. Choose Layer > Layer Style > Scale Effects. Turn on the Preview option and enter a Scale value. Click OK when you are satisfied with the result. You must repeat the scaling for each layer that contains a layer style. For example, if you used the Recessed Type technique, you would scale the type layer and the Inner Texture layer.

Preset layer style applied

Layer effects scaled to 30%

23 | Scratchboard type

Remember when you were in grade school and you created artwork by scratching a design onto a wax crayon drawing covered with black paint? This technique is the digital version of that style of illustration. First, make a soft-colored paint layer. Then cover it with a black layer and proceed to scratch out a design. You can vary this method of using outlined type as a guide and use any outlined selection, or you can skip the outline altogether if you want your drawing to be free-form. Be sure to use the History palette to take snapshots along the way so that you can undo mistakes without losing all of your work.

Background painting

1   Create a new file. Select the gradient tool in the toolbox. Display the Gradient Editor dialog box by clicking the gradient swatch in the tool options bar. Select or create a gradient and click OK.

This example uses a rainbow background that began with the Spectrum gradient.

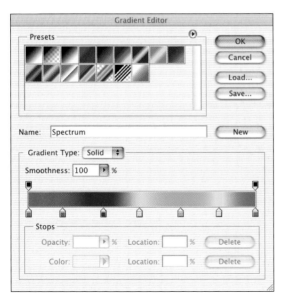

Select a gradient or create a new one

2   Select the linear gradient tool in the tool options bar and drag the gradient tool across the width of the page to fill the entire image area with the gradient.

Fill the page with the gradient

3   Choose Filter > Distort > Ripple to smear the colors. Choose Large and set the Amount to 999%. Click OK.

4   Choose Filter > Distort > Twirl to mix the colors even more. Set the angle to 999°.

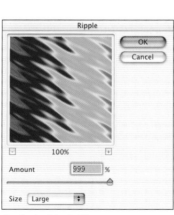
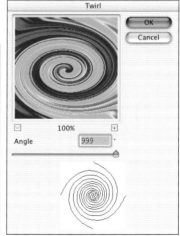

Apply the Ripple filter   *Apply the Twirl filter*

5   Choose Filter > Distort > Wave to distort the gradient completely. Play with the Number of Generators option

until you like the effect. Use Sine as the Type and select the Repeat Edge Pixels option. Click the Randomize button until the image is well distorted. Click OK.

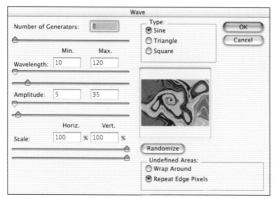

Apply the Wave filter

6   Choose Filter > Wave to apply the filter again. Repeat this step until the colors have been well mixed. To reapply the last used filter without opening the dialog box, press Command/Ctrl+F.

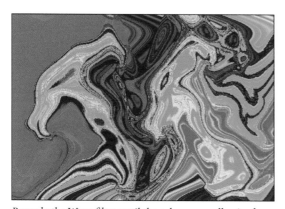

Reapply the Wave filter until the colors are well-mixed

7   Choose Filter > Blur > Gaussian Blur to soften the colors and remove any sharp edges or abrupt color transitions. Adjust the Radius amount until no hard edges remain between colors.

Dispersing colors with the Wave filter

The settings used when you apply the Wave filter can drastically change the look of your background image. To keep a swirly, liquid look to it, start with the settings in step 5 of the Background Painting technique. To bring more color into the edge areas, choose Wrap Around. To break up the color, increase the amplitude.

Original image

Repeat Edge Pixels selected

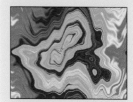

Wrap Around selected

Amplitude increased

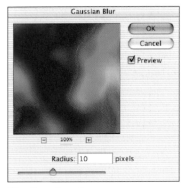

Blur the color edges

8   Edit the background image if needed so that it looks as if it were created with chalk pastels or watercolors.

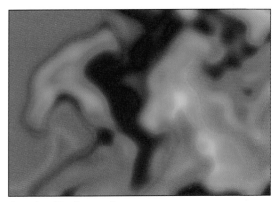

Completed background

Scratchboard type

1   Add a new layer and name it Black. Fill the layer with 100% black.

2   Add another new layer and name it Type Outlines.

This layer will contain an outlined version of the type you will use as a guide in step 8.

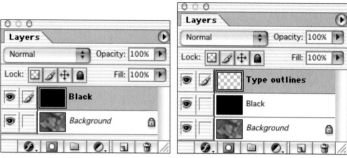

Create the Black layer   *Create the Type Outlines layer*

3   Select one of the type mask tools and use it to create a type selection.

Create a type selection

4   Select a bright yellow color in the Color palette.

This example used a mix of R = 255, G = 255, B = 0.

5   With the Type Outlines layer selected, choose Edit > Stroke. Stroke the type with 1 pixel and choose Outside as the location. Click OK, and deselect the type.

Saving history states in a separate file

Using the History palette is great for creating your work in stages. If you make a mistake you can step backward in history with the History palette. You do this by clicking on a history state or a snapshot. However, closing the file deletes all snapshots and history states. If you want to save a particular history state or snapshot, you save it as a separate file. Select the state that you want to save and click the New Document button at the bottom of the History palette. Save the duplicate file.

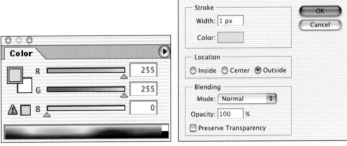

Select a bright foreground color   *Stroke the type selection*

6   Select the eraser tool in the toolbox. In the tool options bar, set the Mode to Brush and the Opacity to 100%. Select a 1-pixel paintbrush in the Brushes palette.

These are good settings to start with, but you may want to experiment with other brushes and modes once you've mastered the technique.

7   Choose View > History or click its tab to display the History palette. Click the New Snapshot button to record the current state of the file.

It's a good idea to take snapshots as you go along so that you can undo mistakes without having to completely redo the entire file each time.

Create a snapshot before scratching

8   Select the Black layer and begin scratching the black with the eraser tool using the type outlines as a guide. Hide and show the Type Outlines layer to view the results as you progress.

In this example, the whole letter was scratched in one direction.

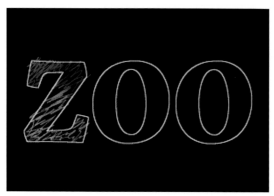

Scratch the Black layer

9 Scratch the letterforms crosswise to give them more weight and a better defined shape.

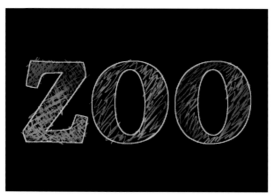

Scratch the letters crosswise

10 Continue to scratch away the black until you are satisfied with the result. Hide the Type Outlines layer. When you are satisfied with the result, save the file.

Creating a tapered brush for scratching

Using a tapered brush with a pressure-sensitive tablet can create some very expressive scratch marks when using the scratchboard technique. Even if you don't have a pressure-sensitive tablet, you can still use the Fade settings to create a tapered brush stroke. If you plan to do much painting with Photoshop, a pressure-sensitive tablet is a must.

To create the tapered brush used in "Scratching options" on page 201, follow these steps.

1 Open the Brushes palette.
2 Select the Hard Round 3 pixel brush. Change the brush diameter to suit your needs. The resolution of your file may affect the size of the brush. The size used in "Scratching options" on page 201 was 4 pixels.
3 Click the name Shape Dynamics in the Brushes palette. Use the following settings: Size Jitter = 51%, Control = Fade (50 steps), and Minimum Diameter = 23%.
4 Click the name Other Dynamics in the Brushes palette. Use these settings: Flow Jitter = 0% and Control = Fade (50 steps).

Hide the type outlines to view the results

Variation: Altered background color

Try this variation to change the background color.

1 Select the Black layer and click the Lock Transparent Pixels button in the Layers palette.

2 Then fill the layer with another color.

In this example, the layer was filled with white.

Change the Background layer to another color

Variation: Altered type color

This variation shows how to change the color of your type but maintain the same background color.

1   Click the Background layer in the Layers palette. Click the New Adjustment Layer button at the bottom of the Layers palette.

2   Choose Hue/Saturation. Turn on the Preview option and drag the Hue, Saturation, or Lightness sliders until you are satisfied with the result.

In this example, the Hue slider was moved to +180.

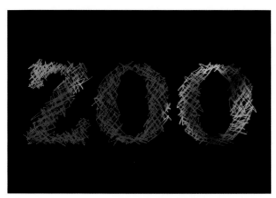

Alter the letter colors with the Hue/Saturation command

Scratching options

Compare and choose from one of these scratching styles. See "Creating a tapered brush for scratching" on page 199 to learn how to make a tapered brush.

Tapered brush

Crosshatched tapered brush

Click once at the start of the brush stroke. Shift-click at the endpoint for a straight stroke.

Constrained tapered brush

Command/Ctrl-click the Type Outline layer to create selection. Select the Black layer and press Delete/Backspace.

Crosshatched and outlined

24 | Type masks

Type masks are easy to create and edit, thanks to layers and grouping. How to save the type depends on the final destination of the image. If you plan to use the file for a Web graphic, you'll want to rasterize the the type. If you'll print the file, you'll want to leave the type unrasterized. If you plan to share the file, you may want to convert the type to outlines to avoid problems if others don't have the proper fonts; but before converting the type, save the original file so that you can edit the type if needed. With any of these methods, heavy sans-serif typefaces usually make the best-looking masks.

1   Open the image that will be masked by type.

Open an image

2   Select the type tool, and create the type that will mask the image. Press Return/Enter or click the Commit button in the tool options bar to commit the changes to the type layer.

For optimal legibility of the type and image, use a large, bold typeface. Thin typeface designs tend to lose their shape when filled with an image, and often the image within is unrecognizable.

What typefaces work well as masks?

Best typeface designs for masks are:
- Sans serif
- Bold, heavy, or black styles
- Simple designs

What typefaces don't work well as masks?

For best results, don't use these typefaces for masks:
- Ornate script faces
- Light, thin, or condensed styles
- Highly stylized or illustrative designs
- Faces with delicate serifs

Create the type that will mask the image

3 Select the type layer in the Layers palette, and move it below the image layer. The type is now hidden by the image. Option/Alt-click the line between the type and image layers to create a layer group.

Even though the layers are now grouped, you can still edit the type or move the image around.

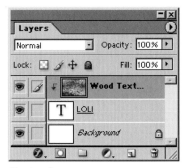

Create a layer group

4 Use the move tool to adjust the position of the image in relation to the type mask. When the image is positioned properly within the type, link the layers. Linking lets you move the two layers around without losing the relationship between them. Save the file.

Adjust the image within the mask

Variation: Inverted image mask

You can give your design a mirror-like depth by placing the masked type on a background of the inverted image that you're masking.

1   Duplicate the image layer, and drag it below the type layer so that the image layer isn't part of the layer group.

2   Create a Hue/Saturation adjustment layer, and use the Colorize option to change the overall color of the image.

3   To invert the image layer, select it, and choose Image > Adjustments > Invert.

You can also create this variation without inverting the image: Just change the coloration of the image or use a filter on it. You can also make a grayscale version of the image so that the area masked by the type pops out in color.

Shortcut: Get the move tool from the keyboard

You can access the move tool from the keyboard when most other tools are selected. Hold down Command/Ctrl to access the move tool. This technique does not work with the pen tools or the anchor point tools. Also, when a type selection is still active, move the pointer outside of the active type area to activate the move tool. You can then click and move the type while it is in edit mode.

Shortcut: Change the type color

Quickly change the color of all the type on a layer by simply selecting the type layer in the Layers palette. Choose a foreground color in the Color palette. Now press Option/Alt+Delete/Backspace to fill the type layer. Only the type is affected by this operation because for type layers, the Lock Transparent pixels option is set by default.

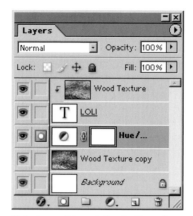

Colorize and invert the duplicate layer

4   Link the new background file and its adjustment layer to the type layer. Linking maintains perfect registration between the type and the background image if you move either of them.

This example shows a simple drop shadow added to make the type stand out.

Completed inverted background image

Vector versus raster masks

Before you start creating a type mask, decide whether you want to use vector (PostScript outlines) or raster (bitmap shapes) masks for the type. This technique starts with the typeface (vector) for the clean, crisp edges that PostScript typefaces and printers can deliver. Compare the edge quality of the graphics in the illustrations. Both images are shown at the same resolution. The vector typeface outline is created from Bézier curves, and will always be smooth and sharp no matter what the printer or file resolution. The raster edge is anti-aliased and slightly jagged and fuzzy. If your graphic will be viewed on-screen and never printed or won't need special typographic adjustments, you may want to convert the type to raster shapes.

Raster mask edge   *Vector (or type) mask edge*

To convert a typeface to vector outlines or to raster shapes, do the following:

1   If you want to be able to edit the type, choose File > Save As and save a copy of the file for later use.
2   Select the type layer that you want to outline.
3   Choose an option:
    • To change the typeface to vector outlines, choose Layer > Type > Convert to Shape.
Photoshop converts the type layer into a shape layer with a vector mask. The vector mask consists of paths that create the shape of the type. These paths now can be edited only with the path editing tools.
    • To change the typeface to raster shapes, choose Layer > Rasterize > Type. Photoshop converts the type layer into a single layer with the type on a transparent background. The type can now be edited only with the pixel editing tools.

25 Circular text

Shortcut: Create circles precisely

To draw a circle from its center point:
Press Option/Alt+Shift while dragging.

To reposition the circle while creating it:
Begin to draw the circle. Press the spacebar and continue to hold down the Shift key as you drag. When the hand icon appears, move the circle to the new position, release the spacebar, and continue dragging to complete the circle.

To enter a precise value for the width and height:
Click the Geometry Options button in the tool options bar. Select the Fixed Size option.

The tricky thing about placing text around a circle is to get the text at the bottom of the circle to be legible. If you just click a circle path and add type to stretch around the whole circle, the type at the bottom of the circle is upside down. In this technique, you'll make two sets of type. One will arc around the top of the circle, and one will arc around the bottom of the circle.

1   Select the ellipse tool in the toolbox. Draw a circle by Shift-dragging until it is the size you want. You can create a circle path or a circle shape layer, depending on your preference. In the following example, a circle shape layer was created.

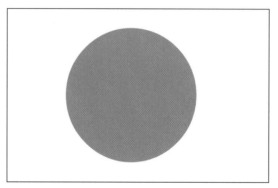

Create a circle path or shape layer

2   Select the type tool in the toolbox. Position the type tool over the circle path at the point where you want the type to begin. Click and enter the type that will appear on the top half of the circle.

3   After you have entered the type, click anywhere in the type and choose Select > All. Press Command/Ctrl+T to display the Character palette. Adjust the size and tracking if necessary.

Add the type that will appear at the top part of the circle

4   To adjust the position of the type along the circle, select the path selection tool in the toolbox. Move the tool close to the X on the path that marks the beginning of the type. The pointer changes to an I-beam with a black arrow. Click and drag the beginning of the type to the desired position.

If you want to move the type to the inside of the circle, continue with step 5. If you want to leave the type on the outside of the circle, skip to step 6.

Adjust the position of the type

5   To create the bottom type, drag the type layer thumbnail to the New Layer button at the bottom of the Layers palette to duplicate the layer. Hide the original type layer.

6 With the type tool, click anywhere in the type and choose Select > All. Enter the type you want at the bottom of the circle. Press Return/Enter to complete the entry.

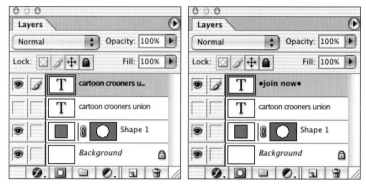

Duplicate the type layer   *Enter the bottom text*

7 To move the type down to the bottom and flip it so that it reads right side up, select the path selection tool in the toolbox. Move the pointer close to the X on the path that marks the beginning of the type. When the pointer changes to an I-beam with an arrow, drag it to the inside of the circle. Once the type is on the inside of the circle, release the mouse button. Click and drag the beginning of the type to the desired position. In the Layers palette, show the original type layer.

Flip the type

8   With the type tool, click anywhere in the bottom type and choose Select > All. Display the Character palette and adjust the baseline shift. Use a positive number to move the type above the circle path. Use a negative number to move it inside the circle path.

In the following example, the top type has a baseline shift of −10. The bottom type has a baseline shift of +3.

Adjust the baseline shift of both bottom and top type layers

9   Once the type layers are in position, complete the image. Change the color of the type, add a layer effect, or add other graphics and images. The following example shows a border, graphic, and layer effect added; the color changed; and the image placed on top of another image.

Add graphics and layer effects to complete the image

Combining layers without flattening

You may need to apply a layer style to a group of layers but don't want to flatten the layers. For example, the button in the image shown in step 9 on this page was created with six layers. If the layer styles (drop shadow and emboss) had been applied to each individual layer, the result would have looked like more than one button. To solve this problem, a separate layer was created that contained a flattened version of all six layers. Here's how it was done:

1   Click the New Layer button at the bottom of the Layers palette to create a blank layer. Move it to the top of the layers you want to combine. Make this your target layer.

2   Hide all layers that you don't want to combine onto the new layer.

3   Press Option/Alt and select Merge Visible from the Layers palette menu.

The new layer now contains a flattened version of all the layers that were visible. You can now apply a layer style to that layer.

The advantage to this method is that you still have all the layers available for editing and changing. If you edit any of the layers, you may have to repeat this technique to make a new composite layer.

Warped and distorted type

Effect	Settings	Procedure
JESSICA	Style: Arc Horizontal Bend = +50% Horizontal Distortion = 0% Vertical Distortion = 0%	1 Create type with the type tool. 2 Click the Create Warped Type button in the tool options bar. 3 Enter the settings and click OK.
JESSICA	Style: Arc Lower Horizontal Bend = −55% Horizontal Distortion = 0% Vertical Distortion = 0%	1 Create type with the type tool. 2 Click the Create Warped Type button in the tool options bar. 3 Enter the settings and click OK.
JESSICA	Style: Arc Upper Horizontal Bend = +55% Horizontal Distortion = 0% Vertical Distortion = 0%	1 Create type with the type tool. 2 Click the Create Warped Type button in the tool options bar. 3 Enter the settings and click OK.
JESSICA	Style: Arch Horizontal Bend = +55% Horizontal Distortion = 0% Vertical Distortion = 0%	1 Create type with the type tool. 2 Click the Create Warped Type button in the tool options bar. 3 Enter the settings and click OK.

There are many, many ways to distort type in Photoshop. You can use the Warp Text command, distortion filters, or the scaling features in the Character palette. The following chart gives you several examples of ways to distort or warp your type. They are not the only ways available, so be sure to experiment to find the one that fits your needs.

Effect	Settings	Procedure
 JESSICA	Style: Arch Vertical Bend = −60% Horizontal Distortion = 0% Vertical Distortion = 0%	1 Create type with the type tool. 2 Click the Create Warped Type button in the tool options bar. 3 Enter the settings and click OK.
 JESSICA	Style: Bulge Horizontal Bend = −50% Horizontal Distortion = 0% Vertical Distortion = 0%	1 Create type with the type tool. 2 Click the Create Warped Type button in the tool options bar. 3 Enter the settings and click OK.
 JESSICA	Style: Bulge Horizontal Bend = +50% Horizontal Distortion = 0% Vertical Distortion = 0%	1 Create type with the type tool. 2 Click the Create Warped Type button in the tool options bar. 3 Enter the settings and click OK.
 JESSICA	Style: Flag Horizontal Bend = +50% Horizontal Distortion = 0% Vertical Distortion = 0%	1 Create type with the type tool. 2 Click the Create Warped Type button in the tool options bar. 3 Enter the settings and click OK.

Effect	Settings	Procedure
JESSICA	Style: Rise Horizontal Bend = +30% Horizontal Distortion = 0% Vertical Distortion = 0%	1 Create type with the type tool. 2 Click the Create Warped Type button in the tool options bar. 3 Enter the settings and click OK.
JESSICA	No settings	1 Create type with the type tool. 2 Display the Info palette. 3 Choose Edit > Transform > Skew. 4 Drag one of the top corners of the bounding box to the right until the angle in the Info palette is –30°. Press Return/Enter.
JESSICA	No settings	1 Create type with the type tool. 2 Choose Layer > Rasterize > Type. 3 Choose Edit > Transform > Distort. 4 Drag any of the corners of the bounding box to create the desired effect. In this example, the top right corner was dragged up and the top left corner was dragged down and to the right. Press Return/Enter.
JESSICA	No settings	1 Create type with the type tool. 2 Choose Layer > Rasterize > Type. 3 Choose Edit > Transform > Perspective. 4 Drag a bottom corner away from the center of the type. Drag a top corner towards the center of the type. Press Return/Enter.
JESSICA	Amount = +80%	1 Create type with the type tool. 2 Choose Layer > Rasterize > Type. 3 Choose Filter > Distort > Pinch. 4 Enter the settings and click OK. Results will vary depend on type size, style and the number of letters.

Effect	Settings	Procedure
JESSICA	Amount = −50%	1 Create type with the type tool. 2 Choose Layer > Rasterize > Type. 3 Choose Filter > Distort > Pinch. 4 Enter the settings and click OK.
JESSICA	Undefined Areas: Wrap Around Use this curve:	1 Create type with the type tool. 2 Choose Layer > Rasterize > Type. 3 Choose Filter > Distort > Shear. 4 Enter the settings and click OK.
JESSICA	Amount = +100% Mode = Normal	1 Create type with the type tool. 2 Choose Layer > Rasterize > Type. 3 Choose Filter > Distort > Spherize. 4 Enter the settings and click OK.
JESSICA	Horizontally scale = 50%	1 Create type with the type tool. 2 Display the Character palette. 3 Enter the settings and press Return/Enter.
JESSICA	Vertically scale = 50% Horizontally scale = 125%	1 Create type with the type tool. 2 Display the Character palette. 3 Enter the settings and press Return/Enter.

Section 4 | Photo manipulation and layering

Watch out

Poison Oak Abounds

BIG SUR, CALIFORNIA · JULY 13, 2003

When you need a soft-edged vignette to frame your image, use this technique to create it. The vignette can be any shape. Use any of the selection tools to create a selection. Then make a layer mask with a blurred edge. To add a soft edge to the whole image, increase the canvas size first, and then follow the steps.

1 Open the image from which you want to create a vignette.

2 In the Layers palette, drag the image layer onto the New Layer button at the bottom of the palette to duplicate the layer. Rename the duplicate Vignette. Hide the original layer.

3 Using one of the selection tools, create a selection that will be the basic shape of the vignette. Reposition the selection where you want it.

4 Click the Quick Mask button at the bottom of the toolbox. Display the Channels palette and double-click the Quick Mask channel to open the Quick Mask Options dialog box. Click the color swatch to open the color picker. Change the color to white and click OK. In the Quick Mask Options dialog box, change the opacity to 100%. Click OK to close the dialog box.

Avoiding sharp edges

To have a smooth gradation on the edge of your vignette, make sure that the area being hidden by the mask is larger than the width of the gradated edge.

In the following two examples, the blur amount was 8.8 pixels, but the masked border is twice the size in the bottom example as in the upper one. Notice how the gradation comes to an edge in the top example. You can avoid this sharp edge either by using a smaller blur amount or cropping out more of the image when making the mask selection.

Masked artwork with 20-pixel border and 8.8-pixel Gaussian blur

Masked artwork with 40-pixel border and 8.8-pixel Gaussian blur

Shortcut: Draw from the center

To draw a vignette selection from the center instead of from the upper left corner, do the following. Select the rectangular or elliptical marquee tool in the toolbox. Position the pointer over where you want the center of the vignette to be. Press Option/Alt and drag to create the selection.

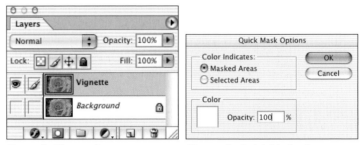

Create the Vignette layer　　　　*Change the Quick Mask color*

Vignette selection in Quick Mask mode

5　Click the Quick Mask channel in the Channels palette to select it. Choose Filter > Blur > Gaussian Blur. Turn on the Preview option and adjust the Radius amount until you like the vignette effect. Click OK.

Be careful not to make the blur radius so wide that it bumps up against the edges of the image. The straight edge will interrupt the soft edge of the vignette.

6　Return to Standard mode either by clicking the Standard Mode button at the bottom of the toolbox or pressing the Q key. In the Layers palette, select the Vignette layer. Then click the Add Layer Mask button at the bottom of the Layers palette to save the selection as a layer mask.

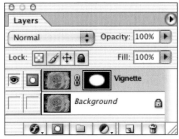

Apply the Gaussian Blur filter   *Save the selection as a layer mask*

7 If you plan to use the vignette in another file, save this file. If you want to add a solid background for the vignette, create a new layer in the Layers palette and move it below the Vignette layer. Select a foreground color in the Colors palette. With the new layer selected, press Option/ Alt+Delete/Backspace to fill the layer with the foreground color. Save the file.

Add a new layer as a background for the vignette

Shortcut: Reuse the same vignette mask

Want to use the same vignette mask on a different image? Select and copy the new image by choosing Select > All and then Edit > Copy. Switch to the vignette file and Command/Ctrl-click the vignette layer mask to load it as a selection. Choose Edit > Paste Into. Photoshop creates a new layer with the new image and automatically applies the vignette layer mask. If you need to scale the new image, choose Edit > Free Transform and scale the image to fit.

28 Framed images

Add a little zest to your image with an interesting frame. It can complement the mood of the photograph or simply help unify and organize a group of images in a graphic way. Following are three different techniques for making frames for your images. You can get a hand-painted effect by painting onto a layer mask. You can make a quick layer mask and then use a couple of filters to create an interesting frame edge. Or you can make a simulated 3D frame by using a shape layer and applying layer styles to it. Each technique is quick and easy to do, so experiment with all three.

Paintbrush frame

1 Open the image you want to frame.

If the image has already been cropped, you may want to add a bit of canvas around it to accommodate the frame. (Do this by choosing Image > Canvas Size and increasing the height and width.) The amount that the frame will cut into the image area depends on the size of brush used for the frame.

Open a file to frame

2 To prepare the image for framing, change the layer properties. If the image you want to frame is the Background layer, double-click its thumbnail in the Layers palette; rename the layer Image and click OK. If the layer is

Using actions to make frames

In a hurry for a frame? Have Photoshop make you one. Choose Window > Actions to display the Actions palette. Click the arrow button to display the Actions palette menu, and choose Frames. Click the name of a frame action, and click the Play Selection button at the bottom of the Actions palette. Sit back and relax while Photoshop creates a frame for your image. Note that the frame actions work best on files with only one layer, so consider flattening the file before running an action. The following images are samples of a few of the frame actions.

Wood Frame – 50 pixels action

Photo Corners action

Waves action

Creating a colored brushstroke frame

Want a paintbrush frame with colored paint strokes? Here's how to do it.

Follow steps 1 and 2 of the Paintbrush Frame technique. Skip step 3 and follow steps 4 and 5. Then finish with these steps.

1 Create a new layer and name it Frame.

2 Select a brush in the toolbox. Choose a color in the Colors palette and paint the frame on the Frame layer.

3 Select the Image layer in the Layers palette. Select the lasso tool in the toolbox and make a selection that falls inside the paintbrush strokes. Click the Add Layer Mask button at the bottom of the Layers palette to mask the image.

not a Background layer, just change its name in the Layers palette by double-clicking the name and typing "Image."

3 With the Image layer still selected, click the Add Layer Mask button at the bottom of the Layers palette.

4 Option/Alt-click the New Layer button at the bottom of the Layers palette to create a new layer. Name it White Base and move it beneath the Image layer in the Layers palette.

5 Choose Edit > Fill. Choose White from the Use pop-up menu and click OK.

The White Base layer will make it easier to view the paintbrush frame as you create it.

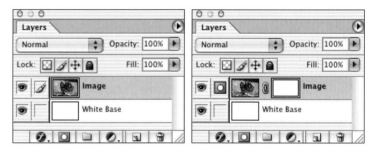

Create the White Base layer   *Add a layer mask*

6 With the Image layer still selected , click its layer mask thumbnail to select it. Select the brush tool in the toolbox. Choose Window > Brushes to display the Brushes palette. Select a brush that has the texture and width that you want for your frame.

7 With the layer mask selected in the Layers palette, paint the edge of one side of the frame.

Paint one edge of the frame in the layer mask

8   If you like the effect, continue to paint the other three sides. To make adjustments, choose Edit > Undo, adjust the brush and try again until you like the effect.

Complete the frame edges

9   To adjust the image within the frame, click the link symbol between the layer mask and image to unlink them. Select the move tool in the toolbox and move the image until you are satisfied with the effect.

Layering brush strokes

To get a layered brush stroke effect like the one in the sample on page 222, do the following.

Follow the Paintbrush Frame technique, except when you start painting the frame in step 7, do the following.

1   Set the opacity for the paintbrush to about 30%. Begin painting the frame.

2   Continue to paint the frame, overlapping brush strokes as you go.

3   Reduce the brush size and continue to paint the areas near the edge of the image until white.

The goal is to create a white outer edge for the image that makes the frame's edge appear sketchy, or painterly, and rough.

Shortcut: Make a white layer in (almost) one step

To create a new layer and fill it with white all in one step, do this. Option/Alt-click the New Layer button at the bottom of the Layers palette. Set the mode to Multiply, select the Fill With Multiply-Neutral Color option, and click OK. In the Layers palette, set the blending mode to Normal.

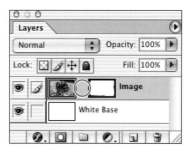

Unlink the layer mask

Move the image within the frame

10 Once the image is positioned within the frame, relink the layer mask and image by clicking the space between their thumbnails in the Layers palette.

Filtered frame

1   Open the image you want to frame.

If the image has already been cropped, you may want to add a bit of canvas around it to accomodate the frame. (Do this by choosing Image > Canvas Size and increasing the height and width.) The amount that the frame will cut into the image area will depend on the size of selection you use for the frame.

Open an image to frame

2   To prepare the image for framing, change the layer properties. If the image you want to frame is the Background layer, double-click its thumbnail in the Layers palette; rename the layer Image, and click OK. If the layer is not a Background layer, just change its name in the Layers palette by double-clicking the name and typing Image.

3   Option/Alt-click the New Layer button at the bottom of the Layers palette to create a new layer. Name it White Base and move it below the Image layer in the Layers palette.

4   Choose Edit > Fill. Choose White from the Use pop-up menu and click OK.

The White Base layer will make it easier to view the frame as you create it.

5   Select one of the selection tools in the toolbox. Create a selection that will be the basic frame shape. With the selection active, select the Image layer in the Layers palette. Click the Add Layer Mask button at the bottom of the Layers palette to turn the selection into a layer mask.

Shortcut: Select and blur the edge at the same time

You can combine the tasks of selecting and blurring an edge by changing the Feathering amount in the tool options bar before you select.

Blurring a selection by feathering is quicker than using the Gaussian Blur filter, but doesn't let you preview or adjust the amount before you make a selection. The higher the feather amount, the softer the edge. The feathering also depends on the resolution of your file.

Experiment with it. Once you've figured out the right Feathering amount, you can make selection after selection without having to use a blur filter.

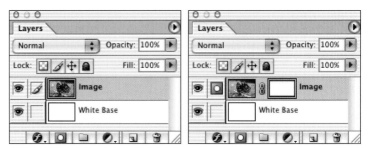

Create the White Base layer   *Make a layer mask from a selection*

6 With the layer mask still selected, choose Filter > Blur > Gaussian Blur. The amount to use depends on the size of the frame and the resolution of your file. The following example uses a Radius of 10 pixels for a 300 pixel-per-inch file.

Using a Gaussian Blur filter introduces more gray pixels to the layer mask. Gray pixels are needed to produce the best results from many of the filters.

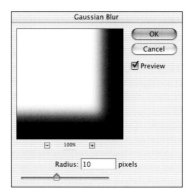

Apply the Gaussian Blur filter to the layer mask

7 Choose Filter > Artistic or Brush Strokes > and select a filter of your choice. The following example used the Spatter filter. After choosing a filter, adjust the settings until you like the texture of the frame. Click OK.

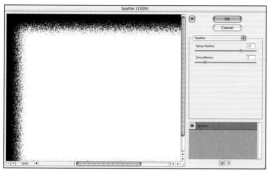

Apply an artistic filter to the layer mask

8 Evaluate the result. If you want to adjust the position of the image within the frame, see step 9 of the Paintbrush Frame technique.

Completed filtered frame

Vector mask frame

1 Open the image you want to frame.

If the image has already been cropped, you may want to add a bit of canvas around it to accommodate the frame. (Do this by choosing Image > Canvas Size and increasing the height and width.) The amount that the frame will cut into the image area will depend on the size of selection you use for the frame.

Open an image to frame

2 To prepare the image for framing, change the layer properties. If the image you want to frame is the Background layer, double-click its thumbnail in the Layers palette; rename the layer Image, and click OK. If the layer is not a Background layer, just change its name in the Layers palette by double-clicking the name and typing Image.

3 Option/Alt-click the New Layer button at the bottom of the Layers palette to create a new layer. Name it White Base and move it below the Image layer in the Layers palette.

4 Choose Edit > Fill. Select White from the Use pop-up menu and click OK.

The White Base layer will make it easier to view the frame as you create it.

5 Choose View > Rulers to display the rulers. Then choose View > Show > Guides. Drag a guide from the horizontal ruler slowly toward the middle of the image. When it snaps into place at the center of the image, release the mouse button. Drag a guide from the vertical ruler slowly toward the middle of the image. When it snaps into place at the center of the image, release the mouse button.

Create guides to find the center point

6 Use the Color palette to select the color for your frame or select the eyedropper tool in the toolbox and sample a color from the image for your frame. In the following example, a blue was sampled from the butterfly wing.

7 Select either the pen tool or one of the shape tools in the toolbox. You will create a frame with this tool. Make sure that the Shape Layers option is selected in the tool options bar. This will be your frame layer.

Select the Shape Layers option

8 Using the intersection of the guides as a starting point, Option/Alt-drag a shape that will define the inside edge of your frame. (If you are using the pen tool to create the edge, just use the guides as a reference.)

Don't worry that the shape fills with color and covers up the part of the image that you want visible. You will correct this in step 9.

Creating different shape layer frames

If you want to use a premade custom shape for a frame, Photoshop has several from which to choose. Select the custom shape tool in the toolbox. In the tool options bar, click the arrow to the right of the shape thumbnail to open the Shape pop-up palette. Choose Frames from the Shape palette menu. Click the Append button to add the frame shapes to the picker. Select a frame shape and follow the directions for the Vector Mask Frame technique. Below are some examples of custom shape frames.

Frame 1

Frame 6

Frame 8

Creating the outside frame edge first

The instructions in the Vector Mask Frame technique tell you to create the inside frame edge first and then the outside frame edge. If you want to create the outside frame edge first and then the inside, use the Subtract From Shape Area option in step 9. You can also press Option/Alt while creating the second shape to get the same effect.

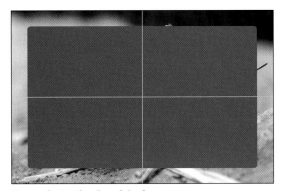

Create the inside edge of the frame

9 In the tool options bar, select the Exclude Overlapping Shape Areas option. This creates the outside edge of the frame and makes the framed area transparent.

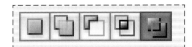

Select the Exclude Overlapping Shape Areas option

10 Using the intersection of the guides as a starting point, Option/Alt-drag a shape that will define the outside edge of your frame. (If you are using the pen tool to create the edge, just use the guides as a reference.) Choose View > Show > Guides to hide them.

Add the outside edge of the frame

11 If your frame goes all of the way to the edge of the image, skip this step. If you need to hide the image area that falls outside of the frame edge, select one of the selection tools in the toolbox. Create a selection area that falls within the frame border. Click the Image layer in the Layers palette and then click the Add Layer Mask button at the bottom of the Layers palette.

Add a layer mask to the Image layer

12 If you want to add a layer style to the frame, select the frame layer (the one you created in step 7) and click the Add Layer Style button at the bottom of the Layers palette. Select a layer style from the pop-up menu. The following example uses a Bevel and Emboss layer style. If you want to adjust the position of the image within the frame, follow step 9 of the Paintbrush Frame technique.

Completed vector mask frame

Shortcut: Quick lassoed frame selections

If you've made a complex frame and the thought of tracing in between its edges is daunting, try using the polygonal lasso tool. For situations where you don't need a precise selection, it's easy to just click, click, click inside of the frame shape. The lassoed area becomes a selection when you reach the beginning point and click.

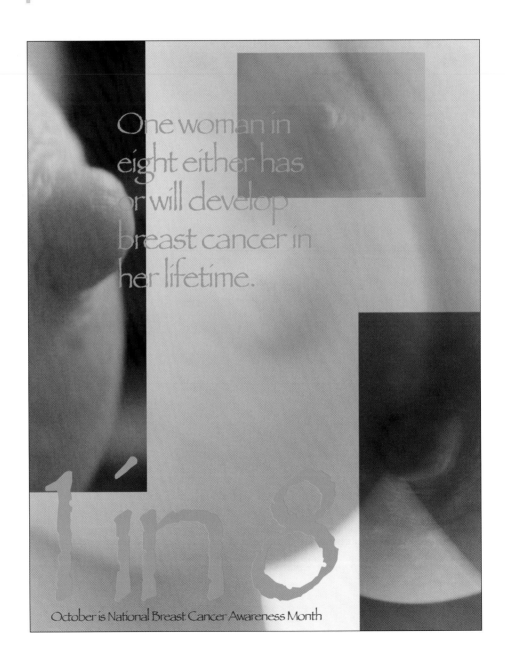

One woman in eight either has or will develop breast cancer in her lifetime.

October is National Breast Cancer Awareness Month

In traditional photography, photographers rely on post-darkroom techniques to enhance black-and-white prints with color. Sepia-toning and iron-toning are two of these techniques; these processes tone the overall print with brown and blue, respectively. Hand-coloring with oil paints is another technique traditionally used to add color to photographs—sometimes to make a print look more realistic and sometimes to create an artistic effect.

Color-tinting

1   Open the grayscale file you want to color-tint. Convert the file to RGB. If you are starting with a color image, choose Image > Adjustments > Desaturate to remove the existing color, or see the tip at right to use Channel Mixer.

Convert a grayscale image to RGB

2   If the image is dark, click the New Adjustment Layer button at the bottom of the Layers palette and select Levels to create a new adjustment layer. Move the histogram highlight and midtone sliders to the left. Click OK.

The goal here is to lighten the image so that you can clearly see the color-tinting.

The best way to convert color to grayscale

Sure, the Desaturate command is quick. But to get the most control when converting an RGB image to grayscale, use the Channel Mixer feature.

1   Either choose Image > Adjustments > Channel Mixer or click the New Adjustment Layer button at the bottom of the Layers palette and choose Channel Mixer.

2   Select the Monochrome option at the bottom of the dialog box.

3   Then enter the following numbers to start from:
R = 24
G = 68
B = 8
These numbers are a good place to start, but you may want to adjust the sliders depending on the values in the image.

If you use a Channel Mixer adjustment layer, you can change it as often as you like.

Painting color onto a grayscale image

You can paint several colors onto one layer over a grayscale image rather than being limited to just one color with a Solid Color layer. Create a new layer and set its mode to Color or Overlay depending on the desired effect (see the following example). Color mode will retain all gray levels in the orginal image and replace them with the color you paint on the layer. Overlay mode is a bit harder to predict but can produce some interesting results. It will multiply or screen the color onto the original image, depending on the color used to paint. Don't worry if you don't like the effect; you can always change the layer mode after you've finished the painting. To lessen the effect, adjust the Opacity in the Layers palette.

Left side: Painted onto Overlay mode layer

Right side: Painted onto Color mode layer

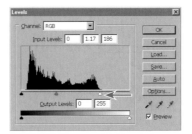

Lighten the image with an adjustment layer

3   Select the area or shape to tint.

This selection has a feather value of 1 because the lips are not hard-edged.

Select the first area to tint

4   Option/Alt-click the New Adjustment Layer button at the bottom of the Layers palette to create a new Solid Color layer. Set its Mode to Color. Click OK.

By setting the blending mode now, you'll be able to see the results while choosing the color in step 5. The Color blending mode allows the layer's colors to overlay the value and texture of the grayscale image beneath it.

Create a new Solid Color layer

5 When the color picker appears, choose a color for your fill layer. If needed, move the color picker away from the image so that you can preview the colors as you sample them.

Notice that the selection is no longer active but has become a layer mask for the fill layer.

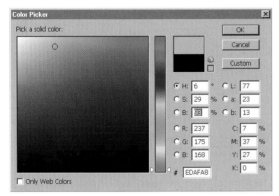

Choose a fill color

6 When you are satisfied with the color effect, click OK.

The good thing about tinting with fill layers is that you can always change the fill color later. To change the fill color, simply double-click the color thumbnail in the Layers palette to display the color picker. Change the color and click OK.

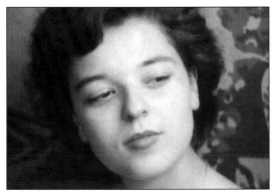

Tinted selection

7 Repeat steps 3 through 6 for each area that needs tinting.

Shortcut: Reset dialog box values

Did you go too far with your Levels adjustment and now want to start over? Don't click Cancel and then reopen the dialog box. You can reset the values in the dialog box without closing it. Simply press Option/Alt to change the Cancel button to Reset. With Option/Alt depresssed, click Reset. Then start over with your adjustment.

This shortcut is available in most of Photoshop's dialog boxes.

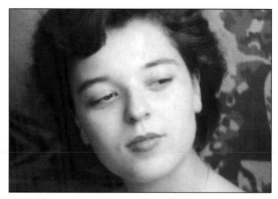

Repeat for each area that needs tinting.

8   Create a new layer and set the blending mode to Multiply. Use a paintbrush or airbrush to add color to areas that are too light or that don't have much original texture.

In this example, more color was added to the right cheek to better match the left cheek.

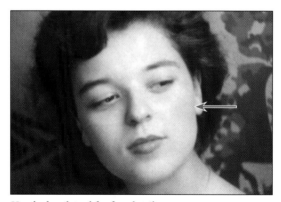

Use the brush tool for fine details

9   As a final step, double-click the Levels adjustment layer that you created in step 2. Move the Levels dialog box so that you can see the image and readjust the contrast level to your satisfaction.

Readjust the contrast level

Sepia- and iron-toning

1   To make a sepia-tone photograph, follow steps 1 and 2 from the Color-tinting technique. Choose Merge Visible from the Layers palette menu. Then choose Image > Adjustments > Variations.

Clicking the variations will gradually change the overall color of the image.

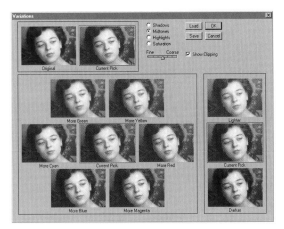

Use Variations to create a sepia tone

Creating a quick sepia-tone

Photoshop often features several ways to do the same thing. Here's a quick way to create a sepia-tone image.

1. Follow steps 1 and 2 of the Color-tinting technique.
2. Option/Alt-click the New Adjustment Layer button in the Layers palette to create a new Solid Color layer. Set its mode to Color. Click OK.
3. When the color picker appears, choose a color for your fill layer. If needed, move the color picker away from your image so that you can preview the colors as you sample them.
4. Select a color and click OK. The values used in the image shown here are R = 180, G = 142, B = 124.

Create a Solid Color layer

Completed sepia tone

Giving your image a quick colorcast

Use Variations to give your image an overall colorcast. Follow the Sepia-toning instructions, but in step 2, use the following color combinations.

Click Green once, Cyan once, Blue once.

Click Magenta twice, Blue twice.

Click Green three times, Yellow once.

Click Yellow five times.

2 Set the slider two notches above Fine.

- To get a sepia tone effect, add Red and Yellow a couple of times. Then add Blue once.

- To simulate iron-toning, click the Blue, Cyan, and Green variations.

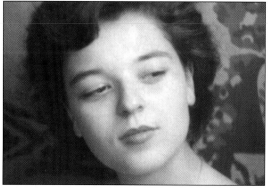

Completed sepia tone

Selective color recovery

1 Open an RGB file and create a snapshot in the History palette. Follow steps 1 and 2 of the Color-tinting procedure.

Open an RGB file

2   Make a new snapshot of the grayscale version. Set the source for the history brush tool to the color snapshot you took in step 1.

Create a snapshot of the grayscale version

3   Create a new layer, select the history brush tool, and paint in the areas that you want to return to full color.

Or if you prefer, make selections and choose Edit > Fill. In the dialog box, choose History from the Contents pop-up menu and click OK. If you make a mistake or paint in too much color, set the history brush source to the grayscale snapshot, and repair the image.

Paint in color areas with the history brush

30 | Collage masks

Sunshine of late afternoon—
On the glass tray
a glass pitcher, the tumbler
turned down, by which
a key is lying—And the
immaculate white bed
   - William Carlos Williams

Photoshop features lots of ways to do many things—and masking images is no exception. In this technique, you'll learn two different ways to mask an image with another scanned image. In both methods, you create a silhouette from the scanned image and use it as the mask shape. Use the Clipping-Group Mask technique if you want to experiment with layer modes and transparency. Not only can the scanned image be used as a mask, but its color and texture can also be integrated into the final effect. Use the Layer Mask technique if you want to play with blending modes or other special effects such as gradient blends between the image and its mask.

Clipping-group masks

1   Using a white background, scan the object from which you want to create the mask.

Use a white background so that selecting it will be easy in step 3.

Scan the object with a white background

2   Preserve the original image by duplicating its layer. Name the layer Mask. Hide the original layer.

3   Choose Select > Color Range to select the white background around the object. Position the eyedropper tool over the white background and click. Use the other eyedropper tools to get a good mask of the entire white background. Click OK.

Fine-tuning a selection with the brush tool

Once you've created a selection with selection tools or the Color Range command, you may want to edit the selection edges. You can add to or remove parts of a selection with the brush tool. You can use any type of brush at any opacity. For example, if you want soft, feathered edges, choose a soft-edged brush.

1. Create a selection with one of the selection tools or the Color Range command, and click OK to activate the selection.
2. Click the Edit in Quick Mask Mode button at the bottom of the toolbox or press the Q key.
3. Select the brush in the toolbox or press the B key. Choose a brush from the Brushes palette.
4. Begin painting to change the selection. Painting with white will add to the selection. Painting with black will remove from the selection. To switch the foreground and background colors, press the X key.
5. Click the Edit in Standard Mode button at the bottom of the toolbox or press the Q key to view the selection marquee.

The only areas that should be selected are the ones that will not be part of the final mask.

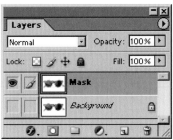
Duplicate the Background layer

Use Color Range to select white areas

4. If the mask shape contains selected areas, deselect them now by Option/Alt-dragging around them with the lasso tool to make a continuous selection. Once you have everything outside of the mask shape selected, press Delete/Backspace to remove the pixels.

In the following example, the small metal rectangles on the glasses were deselected to avoid having two holes in the final mask shape.

Delete the white background

5. Deselect. Create a new layer with the image that will be masked and name it Image.

You can bring layers in from other files by copying and pasting, duplicating layers, or dragging and dropping.

Bring a new image into the file

6 Option/Alt-click the line between the two layers in the Layers palette to group them.

The bottom layer in a clipping group acts as a mask for all other layers within the group. Transparent areas will block out the image above, and areas that contain pixels will reveal the upper layers.

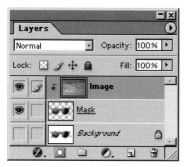

Group the layers to create a layer group

7 Select the move tool in the toolbox, and adjust the way the image falls within the mask. Make the Image layer active, and move it around until you are satisfied with the effect. Save the file.

Shortcut: Manage selections in the Channels palette

To load a selection:
- Command/Ctrl-click the channel thumbnail.
- Click the Load Channel as Selection button at the bottom of the Channels palette.

To add a channel to a selection:
- Shift+Command/Ctrl-click the channel thumbnail.
- Shift-click the Load Channel as a Selection button at the bottom of the Channels palette.

To subtract a channel from a selection:
- Command/Ctrl+Option/Alt-click the channel thumbnail.
- Option/Alt-click the Load Channel as a Selection button at the bottom of the Channels palette.

To intersect a channel with a selection:
- Command/Ctrl+Shift+Option/Alt-click the channel thumbnail.
- Shift+Option/Alt-click the Load Channel as a Selection button at the bottom of the Channels palette.

If desired, add a new layer and place it beneath the Mask and Image layers. This example shows a Drop Shadow layer effect added to the mask layer, and a new Background layer added to the image.

Adjust the image within the mask

Layer masks

1   Follow steps 1 through 5 of the Clipping-Group Masks technique. Command/Ctrl-click the Mask layer thumbnail to load its shape as a selection.

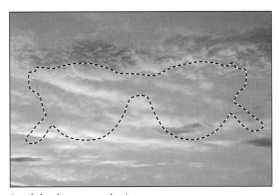

Load the shape as a selection

2   Select the Image layer in the Layers palette. Click the Add Layer Mask button at the bottom of the Layers palette to create a layer mask.

3   Click the link icon between the layer mask thumbnail and the Image layer thumbnail to unlink the two. Click the Image thumbnail.

Layer masks are linked to their layer image by default. Unlinking them lets you move them independently.

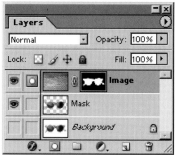 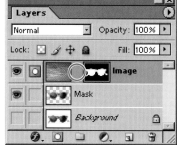

Add a layer mask   *Unlink the layer mask from the image*

4   Use the move tool to reposition the image within the layer mask. When you are satisfied with their relationship, relink them by clicking between their thumbnails in the Layers palette.

Keep the layer linked with its mask so that you can move the two as a group. For a special effect, change the blending mode of the Image layer. The following example shows the blending mode changed to Difference.

Adjust the image within the mask and change the blending mode

Shortcut: Apply last adjustment settings

In one quick step, you can open the Levels, Curves, or other adjustment dialog boxes and start with the last settings.

- To open the Levels dialog box and start with the last settings, press Command/Ctrl+Option/Alt+L.

- To open the Curves dialog box and start with the last settings, press Command/Ctrl+Option/Alt+M.

- To open the Color Balance dialog box and start with the last settings, press Command/Ctrl+Option/Alt+B.

- To open the Hue/Saturation dialog box and start with the last settings, press Command/Ctrl+Option/Alt+U.

EWE
RUMINANT LIFESTYLES

Top ten sheepdips
Woolgathering woes
The headstrong ram

One of the toughest types of images to make is a really good composite. A few tricks, however, help create the illusion that different images from different photos fit together. One trick is to make realistic cast shadows. This technique takes you through the basic steps of how to place an object into a background, adjust its color, and create a cast shadow. You may need to deviate from the instructions for your images. Try different colors for the shadow, or play with different transformation amounts in step 8. If you don't get the gradation angle correct in step 13, keep trying until you're happy with it.

1   Open an RGB image that will be the background for your composite image.

Note the color of the light and the direction of the shadows.

Open the background image

2   Open another file and select the object you want to bring into the background image.

Pay attention to the light color and shadow direction. In this example, the light is coming from a different direction and is much cooler than in the background image. These problems will be corrected later.

Shortcut: Center a layer or selection as you drag and drop

When dragging and dropping a new layer from another file, you can center the image at the same time. Choose the move tool from the toolbox or press the V key. As you drag the layer or selection from one window to the next, press Shift to center the layer in the new file.

Removing edge pixels

Sometimes an object that you copy and paste from another image retains a slight halo that suddenly shows up when placed on a different background. Here are a couple of ways to remove the halo.

- Try using one of the matte commands. Sometimes the results look good, sometimes they don't. You can find the commands by choosing Layer > Matting and then selecting Defringe, Remove Black Matte, or Remove White Matte.
- Make a selection and remove the outer pixels as follows:

1 Command/Ctrl-click the layer thumbnail of the object. This selects only the pixels on that layer, not the transparent areas.

2 Choose Select > Modify > Contract. Enter 1 pixel as the amount and click OK.

3 Choose Select > Inverse to select everything on the layer but the object. (Basically you are selecting the 1-pixel edge around the object.)

4 Press Delete/Backspace to remove the 1-pixel edge.

Select the object

3 Use the move tool to drag the object onto the background. A new layer will be created. Select Layer Properties from the Layers palette menu and name this layer Object. Position the object, and scale and flip the image if necessary. Notice that the red pepper seems to float in the air without a cast shadow.

Drag the object into the background image

4 Option/Alt-drag the Object layer thumbnail onto the New Layer button at the bottom of the Layers palette to create a duplicate. Name this layer Shadow. Select the Lock Transparent Pixels option for the Shadow layer.

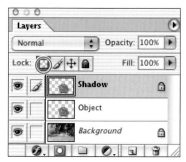

Duplicate the Object layer and lock the transparent pixels

5   Use the eyedropper tool to select a shadow color from the shadows in the background image. If no shadows exist, create a dark color in the Color palette. In this example, a dark color was selected from the shaded area of the bottom of the pepper. Then it was darkened further in the Color palette.

6   Press Option/Alt+Delete/Backspace to fill the Shadow layer with the foreground color.

Because the transparent pixels are locked, only the areas on the layer that contain pixels are filled.

Fill the Shadow layer with a dark color

7   Move the Shadow layer down in the Layers palette so that it is below the Object layer. Turn off the Lock Transparent Pixels option for the Shadow layer.

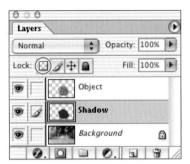

Drag the Shadow layer below the Object layer
and unlock the transparent pixels

8 With the Shadow layer still selected, choose Edit > Transform > Distort. Grab one corner of the shadow to pull it in the direction you want it to fall. Continue to transform the shadow until its shape and angle match the light angle and direction. Make sure that the base of the shadow touches the object that casts the shadow. Press Return/Enter to complete the transformation.

If you are unsure how the shadow should be angled, look at the shadows in the background picture. In this example, the shadow for the pepper was scaled down in height and pulled toward the right to match the shadows for the peppercorns and lettuce leaves.

Transform the shadow shape

9 Choose Filter > Blur > Gaussian Blur. Turn on the Preview option so that you can decide which Radius amount works for your image. When the edges of the shadow look similar in softness to the other shadows in the background layer, click OK.

The Radius amount depends on resolution and existing shadows. Try to match the edge softness of other shadows in the background.

10 In the Layers palette, set the Shadow layer blending mode to Multiply and adjust the Opacity until the shadow is as dark as the darkest area of the other shadows.

The Multiply mode darkens the layers underneath but still lets the texture of the lower layers show through. Don't worry if the shadow seems too dark in some areas. You will adjust it with a layer mask gradient in step 13.

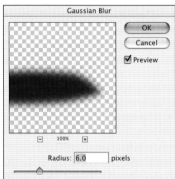

Apply the Gaussian Blur filter

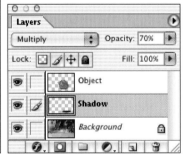

Change Opacity and mode

11 Select the Object layer in the Layers palette. Option/Alt-click the New Adjustment Layer button and drag to choose either Levels or Curves from the pop-up menu. Select the Use Previous Layer to Create Clipping Mask option and click OK.

This adjustment layer will alter the color cast of the object.

Matching the grain of another image

One of the telltale signs of a composite image is different grain textures. Try to match the grain of the images so that the images look natural together.

1 Select the layer that needs to have grain added.

2 Choose Filter > Noise > Add Noise. Turn on the Preview option and select Monochrome. Select Uniform and enter a very small amount. Adjust until the grain matches the texture of the other layers. Click OK.

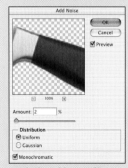

Apply the Add Noise filter

Knife grain matches grain of background image

Adding more shadow realism

Add more realism to the cast shadow by adding a smaller, darker shadow to the large soft one.

1 Drag the Shadow layer onto the New Layer button at the bottom of the Layers palette to duplicate the layer.

Object with one shadow

2 Set the Opacity to 100% and click the layer mask thumbnail to select it.

3 Select the gradient tool. Click the triangle next to the gradient swatch to open the Gradient pop-up palette. Select the Black, White gradient and draw a shorter gradient than the one in the original Shadow layer mask.

Create a new mask gradient

Object with two shadows

Create an adjustment layer

12 Turn on the Preview option in the Levels or Curves dialog box. Adjust the shadows and highlights so that the image appears to fit naturally into the background's lighting.

In this example, the Blue curve was adjusted so that the image would seem warmer and its highlights would look more yellow.

Adjust the color cast of the object

13 Select the Shadow layer in the Layers palette and click the Add Layer Mask button at the bottom of the Layers palette. Select the gradient tool. Click the triangle next to the gradient swatch to open the Gradient pop-up palette. Select the Black, White gradient. Apply a linear gradient to the layer mask with white at the base of the shadow and dark gray at the far edge.

The shadow will fade in the direction of the gradient vector. If the gradient makes the shadow too subtle, reapply using a lighter part of the gradient.

14 With the Shadow layer selected in the Layers palette, click the link box next to the Object layer and its adjustment layer to link the layers.

Linking the layers ensures that any moves or transformations will not separate the object from its shadow. In this example, the pepper and its shadow were scaled down a bit.

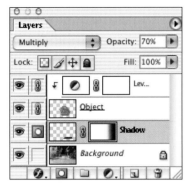

Create a layer mask for the Shadow layer

15 Select the Object layer in the Layers palette. Use the dodge or burn tool to correct other small lighting problems.

In this example, several additional adjustments were made to the image. The stem and the right bottom side of the pepper were darkened using the Multiply Layer tip (see right column, this page). A second cast shadow was added (see "Adding more shadow realism" on page 254). The cast shadow color was changed to incorporate more red so that it looked like a bit of reflective light from the pepper. The Levels adjustment layer was reopened and adjusted to warm up the pepper highlights.

Make small color and lighting adjustments

Subtly deepening or lightening with blending modes

Sometimes you don't want to just darken a color, you want to deepen it. Try this method for a different effect from using the dodge and burn tools.

To deepen the color of an area:

1 Duplicate the layer that contains the area that needs deepening. Set its mode to Multiply.
2 Option/Alt-click the Add Layer Mask button to add a black layer mask.
3 Select the brush tool and set the foreground color to white. Paint the layer mask in the areas you want to darken.

To lighten an area:
Follow the instructions for deepening an area, except in step 1, set the layer mode to Screen or Lighten.

Photoshop offers many, many ways to blend images together. Here are three different ways using layer masks, layer styles, and layer groups. Each one creates a different effect. The easiest to learn and use is layer-mask blending: Create a gradient layer mask to blend smoothly from one layer to another. If you're more adventurous, play with layer-style blending. The results will depend on the images you start with and their highlight and shadow values. And if you want to mask several layers at once without having to flatten them, use the layer-group blending technique.

Layer-mask blending

1 Open or create an image file.

Open an image file

2 Open another file and select the move tool. Position the image windows so that you can see both of them on-screen at once. Use the move tool to drag and drop the image of one file onto the other, pressing Shift before you release the mouse button to center the layer on top of the other layer.

Opening several files at once

Using the File Browser, you can simultaneously select and open all the files you need for a composite.

1 Click the File Browser button in the tool options bar or choose File > Browse to open the File Browser.

2 Scroll through the files and folders in the Folders palette to locate the folder that contains the images you want to use. Select that folder to display its contents.

3 Select the first image by clicking its thumbnail.

4 To select more images, do one of the following:
   - Shift-click adjacent thumbnails to select several consecutive images.
   - Command/Ctrl-click other thumbnails to select random images.
   - Choose Edit > Select All or press Command/Ctrl+A to select all the images in the folder
   - Flag the images you want to use, and then choose Edit > Select All Flagged or press Shift+Command/Ctrl+A to select all of the flagged images.

5 From the File menu in the File Browser, choose File > Open to open the selected images.

Turning a selection into a layer mask

If you'd rather make a layer mask from a selection than from a gradation, follow this method. This technique uses only the selection area or outlines of the selected shape. To use an entire image as a mask, see "Using an image as a layer mask" on page 259.

1 Create the selection.

2 Select the layer that you want to mask, and click the Add Layer Mask button at the bottom of the Layers palette.

Add the layer mask

Composite image

Open a second file

3 With the new layer still selected, click the Add Layer Mask button in the Layers palette. Notice that the foreground and background colors switch to white and black.

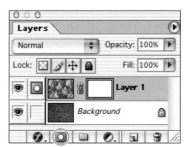

Add a layer mask to the new layer

4 Select one of the gradient tools. In the tool options bar, click the arrow button to the right of the gradient swatch to display the Gradient pop-up palette, and choose the Foreground to Background gradient. Draw a gradient on the layer mask. The white areas of the gradient will reveal the top layer, and the black areas will reveal the layer underneath.

Try different gradients and angles for different effects.

One layer image blended into another

Layer-style blending

1 Follow steps 1 and 2 of the Layer Mask Blending technique.

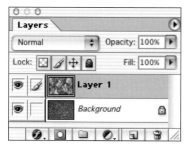

Drag in a new image to create a new layer

2 Double-click the layer thumbnail of the dragged-and-dropped upper layer in the Layers palette to open the Layer Style dialog box. To make the darkest areas of the top layer drop out, drag the black shadow triangle beneath the This Layer slider to the right.

All pixel values that fall into this range will disappear from view and reveal the layer underneath.

3 To soften the transition from layer to layer, split the shadow triangle by holding down Option/Alt and drag one side away from the other. (The triangle turns into two half triangles.) When you like the effect, click OK.

Using an image as a layer mask

If you want to make a layer mask from an image rather than a gradation, here's how.

1 Select the layer that you want to mask and click the Add Layer Mask button at the bottom of the Layers palette.

2 Select the image or object and choose Edit > Copy to copy the image you will use as a layer mask. Deselect.

Copy the image

3 Select the layer that you want to mask and click the Add Layer Mask button at the bottom of the Layers palette.

4 Choose Edit > Paste to add the image to the layer mask. Click the layer thumbnail to view the result.

Add the image to the layer mask

Composite image

Compositing with layer blending modes

An easy way to combine images on different layers is simply to change the layers' blending modes. The results depend on the colors of the layers being blended, so you won't be able to reproduce the following results precisely. But these examples give you an idea of what to expect. Only the blending modes that work best for collage-type imagery are shown here. (For a description of each mode, see the *Adobe Photoshop CS User Guide* or online Help.) In the following examples, the butterfly fabric layer is above the water layer.

Original images

Multiply

Lighten

(Continued on next page)

The lower layer is now revealed through the darkest areas of the upper layer.

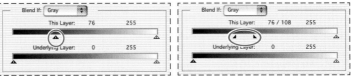

Move the shadow triangle   *Option/Alt-drag the triangle to soften the transition*

4   If desired, edit and re-edit by double-clicking the layer to display the Layer Style dialog box and making additional adjustments.

Lower layer revealed through the dark areas of the upper layer

5   To make the lower layer show through the highlight areas of the upper layer, open the Layer Style dialog box again. Reset the black shadow slider to 0. Move the white highlight triangle for the This Layer slider to the left. Option/Alt-drag the triangle to split it for a smoother image transition.

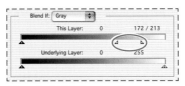

Move the highlight triangle

6 When you are satisfied with the preview, click OK.

The result shows the lower image revealed through the lightest values of the upper image.

Lower layer revealed through the light areas of the upper layer

7 Change the blending mode of the upper layer for a different effect.

In this example, the upper layer's blending mode was set to Difference with the Blend If options set to the values used in step 5. The water texture shows through in the darker areas, and the water image appears in the lighter areas, for a batik-like effect.

Difference blending: Lower layer revealed through the light areas of the upper layer

Compositing with layer blending modes *(Continued)*

Overlay

Soft Light

Hard Light

Difference

Color

Layer-group blending

1 Open a file that has two or more layers. One of the layers should have a silhouette or shape that you want to use as a mask for one or more of the other layers. Position the silhouette or shape layer below the layers it will mask.

This example uses two butterflies.

2 Option/Alt-click the line between each of the layers you want to group. The thumbnail becomes indented, and the base layer name is underlined to remind you that the base layer masks the layers above it.

Once the layers are grouped with that base layer, the other layers adopt the transparency mask of the base layer.

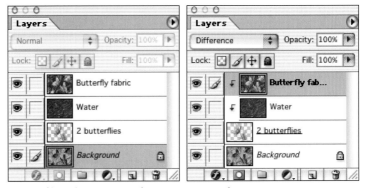

Open a file with two or more layers   *Create a layer group*

In this example, the two layers that make the batik image created in the preceding step 7 are masked by the two butterflies. The Background layer is now the lowest layer and is not part of the layer group.

Upper layers revealed through the layer group base layer (two butterflies)

Variation: Semitransparent base layer

The image you use for the base layer of a clipping group does not have to be a solid shape. Any part of the base layer that has a solid pixel on it will reveal the layers that are grouped with it. Any part of the base layer that is transparent will block out the layers grouped with it. Thus, using an image that fades from solid to transparent will add a soft edge to the layer group.

In this example, the base layer was created by making a feathered selection on a transparent layer and filling it.

Upper layers revealed through the layer group base layer (frame with feathered edge)

Section 5 | Special effects

33 | Posterized photographs

Posterizing colors produces strong, compelling images—and sometimes unexpected results because Photoshop posterizes each channel of a color image. A two-level posterization, for example, produces two colors in each channel of an image, generating a total of eight colors in an RGB image (2 x 2 x 2). (See "Posterizing Grayscale Versus RGB Files" on page 273 for more information.) Because you first convert the image to grayscale, this technique gives you more control over the colors and the number of colors, and lends itself well to process or custom color inks.

1   Open the image that you want to posterize.

Open an image

2   Duplicate the Background layer and name the new layer Smart Blur.

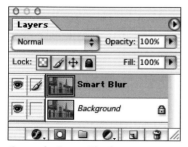

Create the Smart Blur layer

Shortcut: Duplicate and name a layer

Instead of using the Layers palette menu to duplicate a layer, simply Option/Alt-drag the layer thumbnail onto the New Layer button at the bottom of the Layers palette. When the dialog box opens, name the layer and click OK.

You can easily rename a layer by double-clicking its name and typing in the new one.

Blurring predictably with Smart Blur

Smart Blur is great for smoothing the texture of an image while maintaining the edges. Here are a few things to remember:

- A good rule of thumb is to keep the Radius to Threshold ratio pretty even.
- A high Radius to Threshold ratio results in more texture.
- A high Threshold to Radius ratio results in more blurring.

Radius = 20, Threshold = 20

Radius = 100, Threshold = 100

Radius =5 0, Threshold = 100

Radius = 100, Threshold = 50

3 Choose Image > Adjustments > Channel Mixer to remove the color from the Smart Blur layer. Select the Monochrome option. Turn on the Preview option and move the color sliders until you have good contrast and definition of the important shapes in your image.

4 Choose Filter > Blur > Smart Blur to remove the detail and flatten out the gradations. Start with the Radius and Threshold values shown here, and then adjust them for your image. Set the Quality to High and the Mode to Normal.

The goal here is to remove most of the texture and end up with flat shapes.

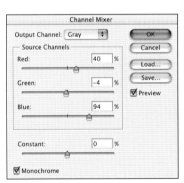

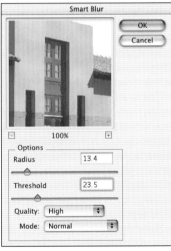

Use the Channel Mixer to remove color

Apply the Smart Blur filter

5 Duplicate the Smart Blur layer and name it Posterized. You will now posterize this layer.

Save the Smart Blur layer intact because you may want to experiment with different posterization levels later.

6 Choose Image > Adjustments > Posterize. Turn on the Preview option so that you can see the effect.

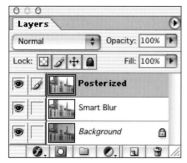

Create the Posterized layer

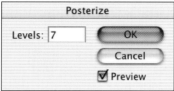

Posterize the layer

Shortcut: Switch between brush and eyedropper tools

Touch-up painting is easy when you can access the eyedropper tool while painting with the paintbrush. Simply press the Option/Alt key to get the eyedropper tool. Click once to sample the color you want; then release the keys and resume painting.

7 Select the number of levels of posterization. Try different numbers to see what detail is lost or retained. The goal is to simplify the image into large flat shapes without losing critical detail. When you find the correct level, click OK.

Posterized image, 7 levels

8 Identify areas of unwanted detail, and then select and fill them with the desired shades of gray. You can use the brush tool to cover unwanted areas as well. Continue with this process until you are ready to add the color.

This example shows the white areas on the face of the building filled in.

Creating colors that match the tonal value of gray pixels

To precisely match the value of the gray pixels in your posterized image, follow these steps.

1 Use the Color palette menu to change the Color palette sliders to HSB sliders.

2 Select the eyedropper tool in the toolbox and click the color you want to change.

3 Note the percentage of the brightness (B) value. The hue (H) and saturation (S) will be set to 0.

4 To create a color of the same value, move the H slider to the hue you desire.

5 Move the S slider to 100%. You now have a color \ equal in value to the gray that you sampled in step 2.

Touch up the image

9 Select the magic wand tool in the toolbox. In the options bar, set the Tolerance to 0. Turn off both the Anti-aliased and Contiguous options. Click a light gray shape to select all the light gray pixels in the image.

In this example, the area clicked was the light gray that defines the face of the building. The magic wand tool then selected all the pixels of that value.

Note: If you don't want to fill all of the light gray pixels in the image with the same color, turn on the Contiguous option, and then Shift-click to select multiple areas before continuing to step 10.

Set the parameters for the magic wand tool

10 Use the Color palette to select the color that will replace the gray, and press Option/Alt+Delete/Backspace to fill the selection.

For more predictable results, try to match the tonal value of the color to that of the selected gray value.

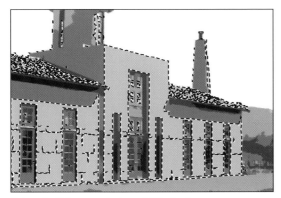

Select the light gray pixels and fill selection

11 Repeat steps 9 and 10 to select a second shade of gray and change its color throughout the picture.

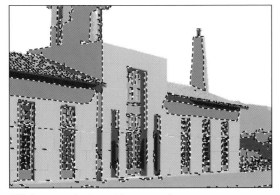

Fill the new selection with a new color

12 Repeat steps 9 and 10 until all the shapes are filled with a color. Use the pencil or brush tool to retouch areas that are distracting.

This example shows bits of texture in the foreground area painted over.

Creating tints and shades with the Color palette

When your Color palette sliders are set to RGB, it can be difficult to select different values of similar colors. To make this job easier, use the Color palette menu to switch to the HSB sliders.

For example, if you want to use different tints and shades of a certain blue, switch to the HSB sliders. Select the hue with the H slider. For tints (white added to a color), reduce the saturation with the S slider. For shades (black added to a color), reduce the brightness with the B slider. For tones (white and black added to a color), adjust both S and B sliders.

Basic hue selected

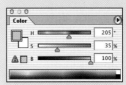

Saturation reduced for tint

Brightness reduced for shade

Completed image

Variation: Single-color posterization

If you want an image that is a variation of tones made from one color, follow steps 1 through 8. Then Option/Alt-click the New Adjustment Layer button at the bottom of the Layers palette, and from the pop-up menu choose Solid Color. Select the Use Previous Layer to Create Clipping Mask option and change the mode to Overlay. Click OK.

Create a Solid Color layer

When the color picker appears, try different colors. When you're satisfied with the color effect, click OK.

Posterizing grayscale versus RGB files

Posterizing a grayscale image produces predictable results—just as many colors as the specified number of gray levels. Posterizing a color image produces more colors than the levels specified in the Posterize dialog box. For example, if you posterize a CMYK file to two levels, you will get sixteen different colors in the resulting image. Each channel is posterized to two levels. As the channels overlay each other, they create more colors. To figure out how many colors will result, multiply the level amount (in this case, 2) times itself 4 times because there are four channels. The equation is 2 x 2 x 2 x 2 = 16 colors. Look at the following examples to visualize this better.

RGB file posterized to two levels (eight colors)

Grayscale file posterized to two levels (two colors)

Red channel

Two colors (black and white) in the Red channel equal two colors in the RGB channel (white and cyan).

Red + Green channels

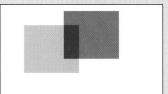
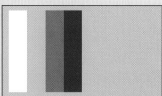

Two colors (black and white) in the Red and Green channels equal four colors in the RGB channel (white, cyan, magenta, blue).

Red + Green + Blue channels

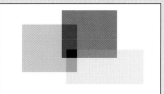

Two colors (black and white) in the Red, Green, and Blue channels equal eight colors in the RGB channel (white, cyan, magenta, blue, yellow, green, red, and black).

34 | Warhol-style images

A prolific painter, Andy Warhol is perhaps best known for his posterized images of soup cans, movie stars, and endangered animals. He used the photographic and printmaking technology available in the '60s and '70s. This technique shows you how to use Photoshop to do what he did. First, open a photograph and use adjustment layers to remove the color and posterize it. You can also selectively burn in or dodge out certain areas of the photo. Once you've prepared the image, you'll add the color. To be true to the Warhol style, use very bright colors. As a final step, add just a few painted highlights to accent certain areas of the image. Following the technique are instructions on how to put your image into a grid of repeated images—another Warhol form for visual impact.

Basic Warhol-style image

1   Open an RGB image. The images that work best with this technique are ones with the subject isolated from the background in some way. If the subject contains similar textures or colors to the background, it will be more difficult to separate the subject from its background in later steps.

Open an RGB image

2   Choose Window > Layers to view the Layers palette. Drag the Background layer thumbnail onto the New Layer button at the bottom of the Layers palette to duplicate the layer. It will be named Background Copy.

Choosing a photo for a Warhol-style image

Look for uncluttered, well-exposed images with the main subject on a plain background. Crop the portraits. Don't show more of the body than the shoulders or bust. The same goes for animals. Usually the entire body isn't shown. These images work well and fit with Warhol's typical subject matter:
• Portrait of one person
• Animals or birds
• Consumer items
You might want to create a composite image with repeated images in a grid.

Shortcut: Switch between the dodge and burn tools

You can switch quickly between the dodge and burn tools. Select one of them in the toolbox. As you work, switch to the other tool by pressing Option/Alt.

3 Click the New Adjustment Layer button at the bottom of the Layers palette. Choose Channel Mixer from the pop-up menu. Select the Monochrome option, and change the Source Channels to the following values: R = 24, G = 68, B = 8.

Don't worry if your image still needs adjustments—you'll come back to this layer later.

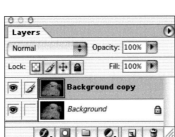

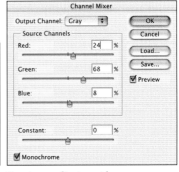

Duplicate the Background layer *Create an adjustment layer*

4 Click the New Adjustment Layer button at the bottom of the Layers palette. Select Posterize from the pop-up menu. Make sure that the Preview option is turned on. Enter a number between 2 and 5. Using a value higher than 5 will make the image look less posterized than Warhol's work. Some of the shapes may blend; you'll fix that in the next few steps.

Posterize the layer

5 Double-click the Channel Mixer adjustment thumbnail in the Layers palette. Make sure that Preview is turned on. Start making small adjustments to the R, G, and B source channel settings to improve the look of your image. Click OK.

In this example, the R and G settings were changed to enlarge the white area around the eye.

Change the Channel Mixer adjustment layer settings

6 Select the Background Copy layer in the Layers palette. Select the dodge tool in the toolbox. In the tool options bar, set the Exposure to about 15%.

Adjust exposure settings for the dodge tool

7 Working on the Background Copy layer, use the dodge tool to lighten areas in the image. Use the burn tool (also set to 15% Exposure) to darken areas of the image.

This example shows the lower beak lightened and the upper beak and lower eye darkened.

Shortcut: Cycle through exposure tools

To cycle through the exposure tools from the keyboard, press the O key to select whichever tool is visible in the toolbox. Then press Shift+O key to cycle through the dodge, burn, and sponge tools.

Shortcut: Adjust exposure from the keyboard

Use the number keys to change the exposure amount from the keyboard. For example, type 1 to get 10%; type 2 to get 20%; type 1 and then 5 quickly to get 15%.

Use the dodge and burn tools to enhance the image

8 Click the New Layer button at the bottom of the Layers palette to create a new layer. Name it Merged Image. Make sure that it is at the top of the layer stack. Turn off the Background layer.

9 Press Option/Alt while choosing Merge Visible from the Layers palette menu. The visible layers will be merged onto the Merged Image layer. Pressing Option/Alt retains a copy of the original layers. Turn off all the layers except the Merged Image layer.

Retaining a copy of the other layers is useful if you want to go back and re-edit the image.

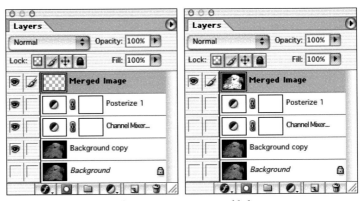

Create the Merged Image layer   *Merge visible layers*

10 Select the magic wand tool in the toolbox. In the tool options bar, set the Tolerance to 0; turn off the Anti-aliased and Contiguous options.

Posterized images have no soft edges, so you don't want the first two options. Contiguous lets you select only one shape at a time. You want to select all of the shapes filled with the same color at once.

| Tolerance: 0 | ☐ Anti-aliased | ☐ Contiguous | ☐ Use All Layers |

Adjust settings for the magic wand tool

11 Click one area of color in the image to select all shapes painted that color. In this example, all of the black shapes are selected.

Use the magic wand tool to select a single-color area

12 Select a foreground color in the Color palette. Press Option+Delete/Alt+Backspace to quickly fill a selection with the foreground color. Choose View > Extras to hide the selection edges so that you can evaluate the image. If you are satisfied with the color, continue to the next step. If not, choose another color and refill the selection until you are satisfied.

Fill the selection with the foreground color

13 Repeat steps 11 and 12 until all the areas are filled with color. If you want to fill a certain shape with color but not fill all of its companion shapes, before selecting, turn on the Contiguous option in the options bar.

In this example, the background was selected separately so that its color wouldn't be part of the eagle's head.

Fill other areas with color

14 As a final Warhol touch, make a new layer and add a few contrasting brush strokes to highlight certain parts of the image. If you have a pressure-sensitive tablet and stylus, you'll get the most authentic-looking results.

In this example, the new brush stroke layer was set to the Difference blending mode.

Add brush stroke details

Different color versions

Many of Andy Warhol's paintings were color variations of the same image. Make one color version, and you can make variations quickly using the Replace Color command. It allows you to change one color at a time while previewing.

1   Follow the Warhol-style Images technique. To preserve the original file, save it, and then choose File > Save As and rename the file.

2   Select the Merged Image layer in the Layers palette.

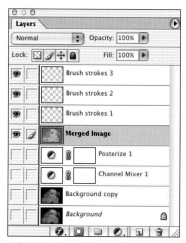

Select the Merged Image layer

Changing colors without selecting

Change the colors in your image quickly without selecting a thing, by creating a Hue/Saturation adjustment layer. The advantage to this adjustment layer is that you can edit it or remove it without permanently changing your image. The disadvantage is that unless you make a layer mask, the adjustment layer will change all the colors on the layer at once. If you want control over individual colors, use the Different Color Versions technique.

1   Select the layer in the Layers palette that you want to change.

2   Click the New Adjustment Layer button at the bottom of the Layers palette. Choose Hue/Saturation from the pop-up menu.

3   When the Hue/Saturation dialog box appears, change the settings until you are satisfied with the result.

4   Click OK.

5   If you want the adjustment layer to affect only the one layer, Option/Alt-click the line between the adjustment layer and the layer in the Layers palette to group them.

3 Choose Image > Adjustments > Replace Color. Use the eyedropper pointer and click the color area that you want to change. Adjust the Hue, Saturation, or Lightness sliders until you are satisfied with the color change. Click OK.

In this example, the background purple color was selected and changed to a teal color.

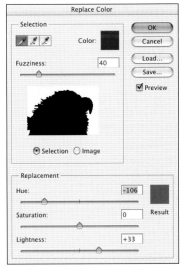

Use Replace Color to change the color

4 Repeat step 3 for each color that you want to change.

Final color variation

Multi-image grid

Many of Andy Warhol's paintings were grids of the same repeated image, sometimes with the same color scheme, sometimes with varying color schemes. You can make a multi-image grid with Photoshop using the Picture Package feature.

1   Choose File > Automate > Picture Package. Select a page size from the Page Size pop-up menu. Select a layout from the Layout menu.

If there isn't a layout that you want, just click a layout that's close to it and you can edit it later.

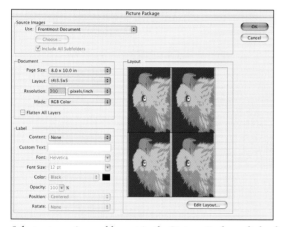

Select a page size and layout in the Picture Package dialog box

2   If you don't need to edit the layout, skip to step 3. If you need to edit the layout, click the Edit Layout button to open the Edit Layout dialog box. Add, remove, resize, or reposition the zones until you are satisfied with the layout. Name the layout in the Names text box. Click Save and name your layout.

In this example, the images were moved and centered on the page with a small gutter between them.

Designing the layout with a grid

Designing a custom layout with the Picture Package feature can be easier if you use a grid. Click the Snap To option to turn on the grid. When you move the image zones around, they will snap to the grid lines. You can change the grid size to as small as 1/4-inch or as large as 8-1/2 inch.

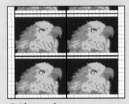

Grid turned on

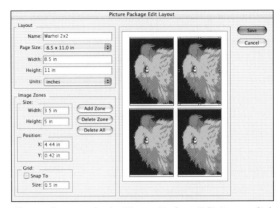

Change the zones, in the Picture Package Edit Layout dialog box

3 If you want to make multiple versions of the same image, skip to step 4. If you want a grid of different images, click the thumbnail image of the file you want to replace. Locate the file in the Select an Image File dialog box that appears, and click Open.

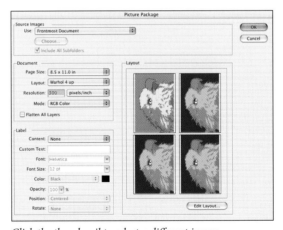

Click the thumbnail to select a different image

4 Once you have selected one or more images for your grid, deselect the Flatten All Layers option.

Deselecting this option places each image on a separate layer in the final Picture Package file. Separate layers give you more flexibility if you want to rearrange the images; you can always flatten the file later.

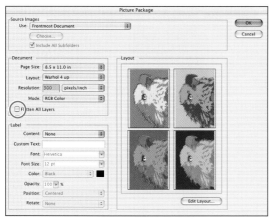

Deselect Flatten All Layers option

5 When you have completed placing the files, click OK. Picture Package automatically opens the files needed and resizes and places them in position.

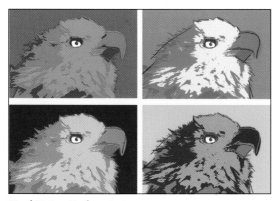

Final Picture Package image

35 | Simulated film grain

Fine-textured grain technique (72 ppi)

Colored grain technique (72 ppi)

Fine-textured grain technique (300 ppi)

Colored grain technique (300 ppi)

Clumpy grain technique (72 ppi)

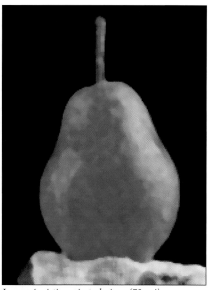

Impressionistic grain technique (72 ppi)

Clumpy grain technique (300 ppi)

Impressionistic grain technique (300 ppi)

Specifying noise options

The Add Noise filter randomly distributes pixels in an image. The pixel size is the same as the pixels in your image (resolution). A value of 72 pixels per inch will produce larger noise pixels than 300 pixels per inch. The Uniform distribution option produces pixels no darker than the percentage amount you enter. For example, the following image uses 10% noise, so the pixels are very pale. Gaussian distribution mixes dark and light pixels. The Monochromatic option adds texture, but not color.

Uniform distribution

Gaussian distribution

Monochrome option

Graininess is a mottled texture created by clumps of silver on photographic film. This quality is usually seen in greatly enlarged photographs or in photographs shot with a fast film speed. This section has four techniques for adding grain to your image. Look at the examples on the previous two pages to see which will work best for your image. It's recommended that you use images that have a soft, ethereal quality or subject matter for this technique. You will end up with a softer, slightly impressionistic or misty image. All filter values used in the examples are the same values used in the technique.

Fine-textured graininess

1   Open the file to which you will add grain. Choose Filter > Noise > Add Noise. Select the Monochromatic option so that only the texture changes and not the color. Enter the desired noise amount. Click OK.

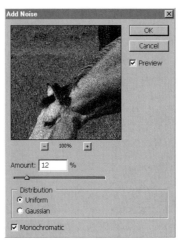

Apply the Add Noise filter

2   Evaluate the result and save the file.

Sometimes the fine-textured grain is quite subtle on a high-resolution file. For a more pronounced effect, increase the amount of noise or try one of the following techniques.

Completed fine-texture grain

Colored film grain

1   Open an RGB file and choose Filter > Texture > Grain. Select the Enlarged grain type. Experiment with the Intensity and Contrast values until you are happy with the preview. Click OK.

The contrast setting will darken the shadows and lighten the highlights in the original image.

Apply the Grain filter

2   Evaluate the result and save the file.

This variation adds new colors to your image. You will see hints of pure Red, Green, and Blue values sprinkled throughout the image.

Shortcut: Zoom with an open dialog box

You can access the zoom tool with the keyboard while a dialog box is open. This is handy when you want to compare the image with a preview proxy in a filter dialog box. Choose one of two methods:

• Move the pointer outside of the dialog box and over the image. Press Command/Ctrl to convert the pointer to the zoom tool for zooming in. Press Command/Ctrl+Option/Alt for zooming out.

• Press Command/Ctrl+ − (minus key) to zoom out. Press Command/Ctrl+ = (equal sign) to zoom in.

Completed colored film grain

Clumpy film grain

1   Open an RGB file and choose Filter > Artistic > Film Grain.
    Start with the values used here and adjust them for your
    image. Click OK.

Apply the Film Grain filter

2   Choose Filter > Noise > Median. Set the Radius to 1 pixel.

The Median filter will soften the grain and make it clumpy.

3   Evaluate the result and save the file.

This is a good technique to use when you want to simulate the
way real photographic grain looks on a greatly enlarged image.

Completed clumpy film grain

Impressionistic grain

1 Open your file and choose Image > Mode > Lab Color.
   Select the Lightness channel in the Channels palette.

The Lightness channel controls the color values in the image
but not the hues.

Select the Lightness channel

2 Choose Filter > Texture > Grain. Select the Clumped
   grain type. Start with these values: Intensity = 29 and
   Contrast = 60, and then adjust them for your image.
   Click OK.

Apply the Grain filter

3 Return to the Lab channel to evaluate the result. Save the file.

The resulting image is the softest and most impressionistic of all of the variations shown. Choose this method when you want the photograph to have a painterly quality, but retain enough detail to look photographic.

Completed impressionistic grain

Choosing the right amounts for noise and grain

The amount of film grain you add to an image will vary depending on the size and resolution of the image, and whether the image will be viewed in print or on screen. If destined for the screen, it's much easier to gauge the amount: base the amount on how the file looks on your screen. However, if you will print the image, keep in mind that the grain effect may change or disappear. If you will print the image on a four-color press, each image will be printed using a halftone screen. That means that the image will be broken up into tiny little dots; so if you added a small amount of grain, it may disappear among these halftone dots. The chart below shows how grain will look at different resolutions.

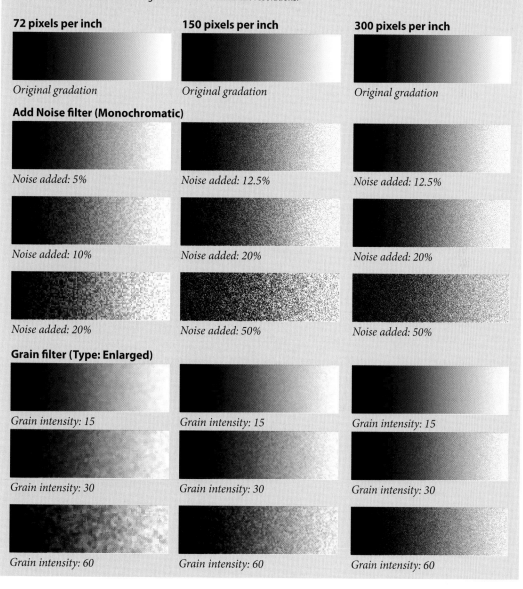

72 pixels per inch

Original gradation

150 pixels per inch

Original gradation

300 pixels per inch

Original gradation

Add Noise filter (Monochromatic)

Noise added: 5%

Noise added: 12.5%

Noise added: 12.5%

Noise added: 10%

Noise added: 20%

Noise added: 20%

Noise added: 20%

Noise added: 50%

Noise added: 50%

Grain filter (Type: Enlarged)

Grain intensity: 15

Grain intensity: 15

Grain intensity: 15

Grain intensity: 30

Grain intensity: 30

Grain intensity: 30

Grain intensity: 60

Grain intensity: 60

Grain intensity: 60

36 | Filter combinations

Original 300 ppi images

Median & Watercolor

1   Choose Filter > Noise >
    Median. Use a Pixel amount
    of 6.

2   Choose Filter > Artistic >
    Watercolor. Use these
    values: Brush Detail = 9,
    Shadow Intensity = 0, and
    Texture = 2.

Some textures and special effects can only be created with the application of several filters. Shown here are just a few of the hundreds of combinations that you can use to enhance images. Although the examples illustrate filters applied to the entire image, these combinations can also be applied to just a selected area. To create an effect shown here, apply the filters in the order indicated. In some cases, you can use the Filter Gallery to apply multiple filters. If you are going to fade one of several filter effects, apply the filter separately from the other Filter Gallery filters to avoid fading the entire set of filters used. Note that the effects may vary with different image resolutions and modes. Use RGB images with these techniques; some of the filters won't work with CMYK images.

Mosaic & Ripple

1   Choose Filter > Pixelate > Mosaic. Use the following values: Cell Size = 10. Click OK.

2   Choose Filter > Distort > Ripple. Use the following values: Amount = 100%, Size = Medium; click OK.

Dry Brush & Rough Pastels

1   Choose Filter > Artistic > Dry Brush. Use the following values: Brush Size = 2, Brush Detail = 8, and Texture = 1.

2   Choose Filter > Artistic > Rough Pastels. Use the following values: Stroke Length = 6, Stroke Detail = 4, Texture = Canvas, Scale = 100, Relief = 20, and Light = Bottom. Click OK.

Pointillize & Glass

1   Choose Filter > Pixelate > Pointillize. Use a Cell Size = 6. Click OK.

2   Choose Filter > Distort > Glass. Use the following values: Distortion = 1, Smoothness = 2, Texture = Frosted. and Scaling = 100%. Click OK.

Note: To have a color other than white show in the background, select a different background color before you start.

Poster Edges & Smart Blur

1 Choose Filter > Artistic > Poster Edges. Use these values: Edge Thickness = 4, Edge Intensity = 2, and Posterization = 3. Click OK.

2 Choose Filter > Blur > Smart Blur. Use these values: Radius = 40, Threshold = 68, Quality = High, and Mode = Normal. Click OK.

Graphic Pen & Palette Knife

1 Set the foreground color to Black. Choose Filter > Sketch > Graphic Pen. Use these values: Stroke Length = 15, Light/Dark Balance = 50, and Stroke Direction = Right Diagonal.

2 Choose Filter > Artistic > Palette Knife. Use these values: Stroke Size = 1, Stroke Detail = 3, and Softness = 5. Click OK.

Dry Brush & Graphic Pen

1 Choose Filter > Artistic > Dry Brush. Use these values: Brush Size = 5, Brush Detail = 8, and Texture = 1. Click OK.

2 Press the D key. Choose Filter > Sketch > Graphic Pen. Use these values: Stroke Length = 15, Light/Dark Balance = 50, and Stroke Direction = Right Diagonal. Click OK.

3 Choose Edit > Fade Graphic Pen. Set the Mode to Soft Light at 100% opacity.

37 Textured 3D graphics

It's easy to add photographic or painterly textures to three-dimensional grayscale graphics using the Overlay mode in Photoshop. The graphic you start with can come from Illustrator or Photoshop. With Illustrator's 3D effects, it's easier to create the graphic in Illustrator and then paste it into Photoshop. But you can also use a Photoshop shape or path. Simply place the graphic on a layer in Photoshop. You then copy a texture onto an adjacent layer and combine the two layers using the Overlay mode. If you have several graphic objects to texturize, it's best to create a separate file for each shape and then combine them in another file using flattened versions of the final texturized graphic. Don't be intimidated by the length of this technique. It's really very easy!

Front-surface graphic

1   Create the intial 3D form. If you create the form in Photoshop, follow the instructions in "Preparing 3D objects created in Photoshop for texturizing" on page 303; then go to step 7 of this technique.

2   In Illustrator, adjust the preferences before copying and pasting paths from Illustrator to Photoshop. Choose Illustrator > Preferences > File Handling & Clipboard (Mac OS X) or Edit > Preferences > Files & Clipboard (Windows). Select the AICB option and click the Preserve Paths option. Click OK.

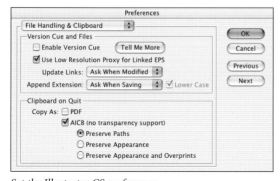

Set the Illustrator CS preferences

Bringing paths into Photoshop

There are four different ways to bring an Illustrator image into Photoshop. Three of those ways (Export, Open, and Place) raster-ize the image. Only Copy and Paste let you use the image as paths or shape layers. Make sure that you have selected the Preserve Paths option in Illustrator's preferences before you copy and paste. See Appendix B, "Combining Illustrator and Photoshop Files" on page 318 for more information on using Illustrator artwork in Photoshop.

3   Create a three-dimensional shape in Illustrator. Paint the shape with shades of gray only. Do not use 100% black or white. Scale the artwork, if necessary, to its final size.

4   If you used the 3D Effect command to create the object, select the object and choose Object > Expand Appearance. Then select all of the shapes and choose Edit > Copy to copy them to the Clipboard. Save the file and switch to Photoshop.

You can create this graphic with the Photoshop shape tools, but it's easier in Illustrator.

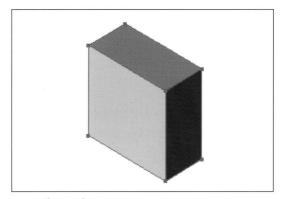

Create the 3D object

5   Create a new RGB file in Photoshop at the size and resolution you want for the final image and name the file 3D Object. Choose Edit > Paste and select the Paste As Path option. Click OK. Do not move the path from its pasted position.

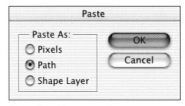

Paste the object as paths

Preparing 3D objects created in Photoshop for texturizing

If you don't own Illustrator, you can still create 3D objects in Photoshop with some extra effort. Follow these steps to prepare the object so that you can proceed with the Textured 3D Graphics technique.

1 Create each surface as a separate shape layer. Make sure that each layer is painted a different shade of gray.

2 With one of the shape layers selected, display the Paths palette to view the Shape layer's vector mask. Double-click the thumbnail in the Paths palette to open the Save Path dialog box. Name the path and click OK.

3 Repeat step 2 for each shape layer. Save the file.

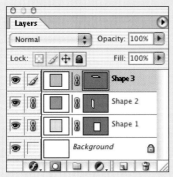

Create sides as shape layers

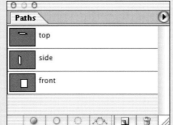

Save the shape vector masks as paths

4 Select one of the shape layers and choose Layer > Rasterize > Shape. Repeat for each shape layer. Link the shape layers by selecting one in the Layers palette and clicking the link area next to the thumbnails of the other shape layers.

5 Choose Merge Linked from the Layers palette menu to create a composite 3D object on one layer.

6 Proceed with step 7 of the Front-surface Graphics technique. Note that you will have separate saved paths instead of all paths saved together, but this should not pose a problem.

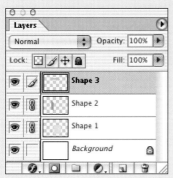

Rasterize and link the shape layers

Merge the linked shape layers

Transforming paths and shape layers

You can transform any path or shape layer with the Free Transform Path command. Select a path or shape layer and use the keyboard shortcut for Free Transform (Command/Ctrl+T). You can then move, rotate, or scale the path or shape. If you want to access the other commands, use the following keyboard shortcuts:

- To distort, Command/Ctrl-drag a handle
- To skew, Command/Ctrl+Shift-drag a handle
- To apply perspective, Command/Ctrl+Option/Alt+Shift-drag a handle
- To display the context-sensitive menu, Command/Ctrl-click the image.

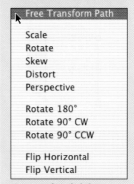

Command/Ctrl-click to display the context-sensitive transformation menu

Turning a path into a selection

There are three ways to turn a path into a selection in Photoshop.
- Command/Ctrl-click the path thumbnail in the Paths palette.
- Select the path in the Paths palette and click the Load Path as Selection button at the bottom of the Paths palette.
- Select the path in the Paths palette and choose Make Selection from the Paths palette menu. This option lets you enter a feather value and gives you options for adding to and subtracting from existing selections.

6 Double-click the work path name in the Paths palette to open the Save Path dialog box, and rename the path 3D Outline. Click the blank area of the palette to deselect the path.

You will use this path several times in later steps to select the outlines of the different surfaces of your object.

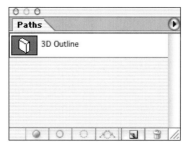

Save the work path

7 Choose File > Place, select the Illustrator file you created in step 4, and click Place. Do not move or scale the object, to ensure that it aligns perfectly with the paths you pasted in step 4. Press Return/Enter to rasterize the image.

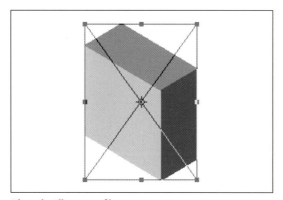

Place the Illustrator file

8 In the Layers palette, select the new layer that was just created by placing the graphic. Double-click its name and rename the layer 3D Base.

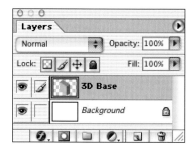

Name the layer 3D Base

9   Open a file with the texture that you want to appear on the surface of the three-dimensional shape. Select the area of the texture that you want to use. Use the move tool to drag the selection from its window into the 3D Object image window.

Open a texture file

10 Using the Layers palette, name the new layer Texture and change its blending mode to Overlay. Option/Alt-click the line between the Texture layer and the 3D Base layer to create a clipping group of the two layers.

You need a clipping group to prevent the Overlay mode from affecting other layers in your file.

About clipping groups

A clipping group is a group of layers whose bottommost layer (the base layer) is used as a mask for the layers above it. The image area on the base layer will reveal the contents of the layers grouped with it.

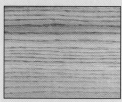

Without clipping group: Texture layer blocks layers below

With clipping group: shape of 3D Base layer masks Texture layer

Distorting the texture on a sphere

Certain textures need a little extra distortion to make them seem wrapped around a sphere. Follow the steps for the Front-surface Graphics technique and then continue with the steps below to make the texturized sphere look more realistic.

1 Complete steps 1 through 10 of the Front-surface Graphics technique.

2 Command/Ctrl-click the sphere layer thumbnail to select its transparency mask. Select the Texture layer in the Layers palette.

3 Choose Filter > Distort > Spherize. Enter a value and click OK. This example used 100%. Deselect and save the file.

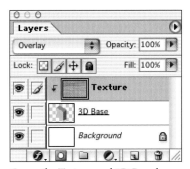

Group the Texture and 3D Base layers

11 Evaluate the result. If your shape has only one visible plane, such as a cone or sphere, and you like the result, save the file. If your shape has angled sides that need adjusting, continue to the Side-surface Graphics technique on the next page.

Areas of the original graphic filled with 50% black will show 100% of the texture. Areas filled with 100% black or white will show no texture.

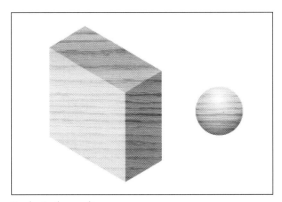

Evaluate the result

Side-surface graphics

1   Drag the 3D Base layer thumbnail onto the New Layer
    button at the bottom of the Layers palette to duplicate the
    layer. Then drag the Texture layer thumbnail to the New
    Layer button to duplicate that layer.

These duplicates will become the side panel. The duplicate
Texture layer will be added to the layer group.

2   Move the 3D Base Copy layer up underneath the Texture
    Copy layer in the Layers palette. Option/Alt-click the line
    between the Texture layer and the 3D Base layer to re-create
    the clipping group. Rename the 3D Base Copy layer Side
    Base. Rename the Texture Copy layer Side Texture.

You should now have two separate, but identical, layer groups.

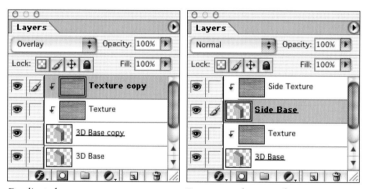

Duplicate layers   Regroup and rename layers

3   Activate the 3D Outline path in the Paths palette. Use the
    direct selection tool to select the path that defines the side
    outline of your object.

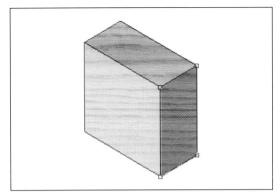

Activate the side path

Using Free Transform on layers

Like the Free Transform Path command (see page 303 inset), Free Transform lets you access all the transform commands with one command. The keyboard shortcut for Free Transform is Command/ Ctrl + T. You can then move, rotate or scale the selection or layer. If you want to access the other commands, use the following keyboard shortcuts:

• To distort press Command/ Ctrl-drag on handle
• To skew press Command/ Ctrl + Shift-drag on handle
• To apply perspective press Command/Ctrl + Option/Alt + Shift-drag on handle
• To display the context-sensitive menu Command/Ctrl-click the image

Command/Ctrl-click and a context-sensitive menu with list of transformation commands appears

4 Click the Load Path as a Selection button at the bottom of the Paths palette to create a selection from the path. Turn off the path by clicking the blank area of the Paths palette to make only the selection marquee active.

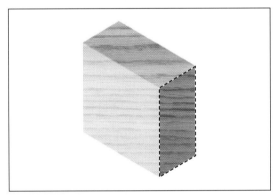

Load the path as a selection

5 Select the Side Base layer and click the Add Layer Mask button at the bottom of the Layers palette.

The layer mask will mask out everything but the side area of the graphic.

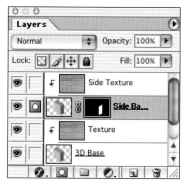

Create a layer mask for the Side Base layer

6 Select the Side Texture layer and select the move tool. Then choose Edit > Free Transform. Transform the texture so that it fits naturally on the side plane of the object. Press Return/Enter to complete the transformation.

In this example, the wood grain was rotated so that it aligned with the edge of the side, and was scaled a bit.

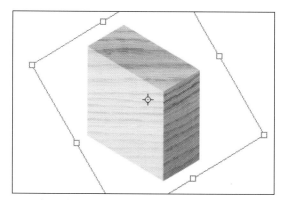

Transform the texture to fit the side

7 With the Side Texture layer still selected, use the move tool to reposition the texture layer. If you are satisfied with the result, save the file. If the top plane of the shape needs adjustment, continue to the Top-surface Graphic technique on the next page.

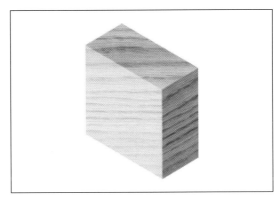

Use the move tool to adjust the position of the texture

Top-surface graphic

1   Repeat steps 1 and 2 of the Side-surface Graphic technique to duplicate the 3D Base and Texture layers. Rename these layers Top Base and Top Texture.

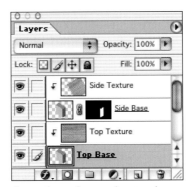

Create the top base and texture layers

2   Turn on the 3D Outline path in the Paths palette. Use the direct selection tool to select the path that defines the top outline of your object.

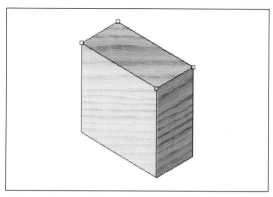

Activate the top path

3 Click the Load Path as a Selection button at the bottom of the Paths palette to create a selection from the path. Turn off the path by clicking in the blank area of the Paths palette.

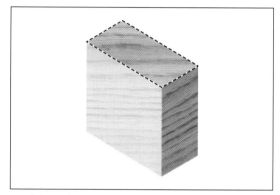

Load the path as a selection

4 Select the Top Base layer and click the Add Layer Mask button at the bottom of the Layers palette.

The layer mask will mask out everything but the top area of the graphic.

Shortcut: Select layers without the Layers palette

With the move tool selected, you can use the keyboard to switch to a different layer with the context-sensitive menu. Control-click (Mac OS X) or right mouse button-click (Windows) an area in the image. A pop-up menu displays the layers that contain pixels in the area where you clicked. Select the layer you want and release the mouse button.

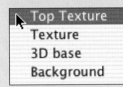

Context-sensitive menu with list of layers appears

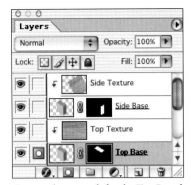

Create a layer mask for the Top Base layer

5 Select the Top Texture layer and select the move tool. Then choose Edit > Free Transform. Transform the texture so that it fits naturally on the top plane of the object.

Scaling the top texture horizontally makes it appear to recede.

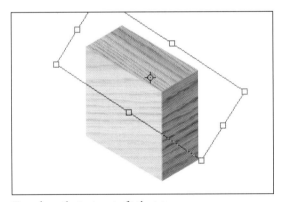

Transform the texture to fit the top

6 With the Top Texture layer still selected, use the move tool to reposition the Texture layer. If you are satisfied with the result, save the file. If the front plane of the shape needs adjustment, continue to step 7.

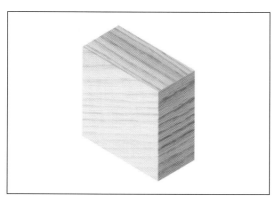

Use the move tool to adjust the texture position

7 Repeat steps 2 through 6 to adjust the front plane of the object, if desired. Use the Texture and 3D Base layers for the front planes. Repeat the entire technique for each three-dimensional shape you want to texturize.

This example shows a gradated cast shadow added.

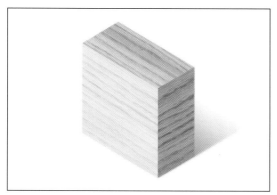

Adjust the front surface

Organizing your layers into layer sets

If you have created an object composed of multiple layers, it is helpful to organize the layers into layer sets. Organizing in layer sets is especially useful if you have several objects made of multiple layers. You can move layer sets around and apply different blending modes to them.

1 Link the layers you want to put into one layer set.

2 Choose New Set From Linked from the Layers palette menu. Name the set and click OK.

This example shows a layer set created for each object.

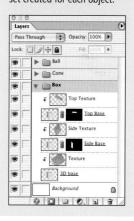

A | Appendix A: Shortcuts

Frequently used shortcuts		
Shortcut	Mac OS X keystrokes	Windows keystrokes
Repeating a task		
Reselect last selection	Shift+Command+D	Shift+Ctrl+D
Use last Levels settings	Command+Option+L	Alt+Ctrl+L
Apply last filter	Command+F	Ctrl+F
Display last filter dialog box	Command+Option+F	Alt+Ctrl+F
Transform with copy	Command+Option+T	Alt+Ctrl+T
Transform again	Shift+Command+T	Shift+Ctrl+T
Transform again with copy	Shift+Command+Option+T	Shift+Alt+Ctrl+T
Moving selected objects		
Leave a copy behind	Option+move tool	Alt+move tool
Constrain movement to 45° or angles set in preferences	Shift	Shift
Move selection area 1 pixel	Any selection+any arrow key	Any selection+any arrow key
Move selection 1 pixel	Move tool+any arrow key	Move tool+any arrow key
Move layer 1 pixel (nothing selected)	Command+any arrow key	Ctrl+any arrow key
Speeding up painting		
Fill with foreground color	Option+Delete	Alt+Backspace
Fill with background color	Command+Delete	Ctrl+Backspace
Get eyedropper while painting	Option	Alt
Select background color (eyedropper)	Option+click a pixel	Alt+click a pixel
Select foreground color (eyedropper)	Click an image pixel	Click an image pixel
Return to default colors	D key	D key

This book assumes that before you try the techniques, you have a basic knowledge of the software and its tools, commands, and palettes. But because you are busy and can't always remember all the commands and shortcuts, this appendix contains most of the shortcuts that you'll need to use this book's techniques most efficiently. Refer to Photoshop Help for a complete list of all the keyboard shortcuts.

Frequently used shortcuts		
Shortcut	Mac OS X keystrokes	Windows keystrokes
Switch fore- and background colors	X key	X key
Display Fill dialog box	Shift+Delete	Shift+Backspace
Decrease brush size	[key (left bracket)	[key
Increase brush size	] key (right bracket)	] key
Select previous/next brush size	, (comma) or . (period)	, (comma) or . (period)
Paint with straight line (any brush)	Click-Shift-click	Click-Shift-click
Cycle through blending modes	Shift+ − (minus) or + (plus) keys	Shift+ − (minus) or + (plus) keys
Set opacity for paint tools	Any number key (e.g., 0 = 100%, 9 = 90%, etc.)	
Show/hide Brushes palette	F5	F5
Show/hide Color palette	F6	F6
Revert	F12	F12
Fill	Shift+F5	Shift+F5
Viewing images		
Toggle between Standard and Quick Mask modes	Q	Q
Toggle between screen modes	F	F
Fit image in window	Double-click hand tool	Double-click hand tool
Magnify 100%	Double-click zoom tool	Double-click zoom tool
Switch to hand tool	Spacebar	Spacebar
Switch to zoom in tool	Command+spacebar	Ctrl+spacebar
Switch to zoom out tool	Option+spacebar	Alt+spacebar
Zoom in on specified image area	Command-drag over preview in Navigator palette	Ctrl-drag over preview in Navigator palette

Frequently used shortcuts for the Layers palette		
Shortcut	Mac OS X keystrokes	Windows keystrokes
Creating and moving layers		
Create and name new layer	Option-click New Layer button	Alt-click New Layer button
Rename layer	Double-click the layer name	Double-click the layer name
Delete selected layer	Option-click Delete/Trash button	Alt-click Delete/Trash button
Create layer from a selection	Command+J	Ctrl+J
Move several layers at once	Link layers before using move tool	Link layers before using move tool
Show/hide just one layer	Option-click eye column of that layer	Alt-click eye column of that layer
Show/hide multiple layers	Drag through eye column	Drag through eye column
Center a layer dragged from another file	Press Shift while dragging layer into window	Press Shift while dragging layer into window
Masks (layer, vector, clipping)		
View layer mask	Option-click layer mask thumbnail	Alt-click layer mask thumbnail
Disable/enable vector mask	Option-click vector mask thumbnail	Alt-click vector mask thumbnail
Discard/apply a layer mask	Drag layer mask thumbnail to Trash button	Drag layer mask thumbnail to Trash button
Create layer mask from selection	Make selection; click Add Layer Mask button	Make selection; click Add Layer Mask button
Toggle between layer mask/ composite image	Option-click layer mask thumbnail	Alt-click layer mask thumbnail
Toggle rubylith mode for layer mask on/off	\ (backslash)	\ (backslash)
Select layer's transparency mask	Command-click layer thumbnail	Ctrl-click layer thumbnail
Turn on/off a layer mask temporarily	Shift-click the layer mask thumbnail	Shift-click the layer mask thumbnail
Make mask on an adjustment layer	Make selection and fill with black	Make selection and fill with black
View mask on an adjustment layer	Option-click adjustment layer thumbnail	Alt-click adjustment layer thumbnail
Create layer mask that hides all/selection	Option-click Add Layer Mask button	Alt-click Add Layer Mask button
Create vector mask that reveals all/selection	Command-click Add Layer Mask button	Ctrl-click Add Layer Mask button
Create vector mask that hides all/selection	Command+Option-click Add Layer Mask button	Ctrl+Alt-click Add Layer Mask button

Frequently used shortcuts for the Layers palette		
Shortcut	Mac OS X keystrokes	Windows keystrokes
Grouping, merging, and copying		
Duplicate a layer	Drag layer onto New Layer button	Drag layer onto New Layer button
Duplicate and name new layer	Option-drag layer onto New Layer button	Alt-drag layer onto New Layer button
Group with the layer below	Command+G	Ctrl+G
Combine visible layers onto new layer	Create new layer; then Option+Merge Visible	Create new layer; then Alt+Merge Visible
Merge down	Command+E	Ctrl+E
Merge visible layers	Command+Shift+E	Ctrl+Shift+E
Make/release clipping group	Option-click line between layer names	Alt-click line between layer names
Create new layer set below current layer/layer set	Command-click New Layer Set button	Ctrl-click New Layer Set button
Create new layer set with dialog box	Option-click New Layer Set button	Alt-click New Layer Set button
Layer styles		
Disable layer style temporarily	Click the effect's Show/hide icon	Click the effect's Show/hide icon
Edit layer style	Double-click layer thumbnail	Double-click layer thumbnail
Edit layer effect/style, options	Double-click layer effect/style	Double-click layer effect/style

Tool shortcut keys

Start using these keyboard shortcuts to access the tools in the toolbox and you'll save yourself lots of time. For tools that occupy the same space in the toolbox, cycle through them by holding down Shift while pressing the keyboard shortcut letter. For example, to access any of the lasso tools, hold down Shift and press the L key until the lasso tool you want to use appears in the toolbox.

Tool	Shortcut key	Tool	Shortcut key
Marquee tools	M	Gradient, paint bucket	G
Move tool	V	Blur, sharpen, smudge	R
Lasso tools	L	Dodge, burn, sponge	O
Magic wand	W	Path selection tools	A
Crop tool	C	Type tools	T
Slice tools	K	Pen tools	P
Healing brush, patch tool, color replacement tool	J	Shape tools	U
		Notes, audio annotation	N
Brush, pencil	B	Eyedropper, color sampler, measure tool	I
Clone stamp, pattern stamp	S	Hand tool	H
History brush, art history brush	Y	Zoom tool	Z
Eraser, background eraser, magic eraser	E		

B Appendix B: Combining Illustrator and Photoshop files

Avoiding color shift problems

Here's a way to avoid color shift problems when you know you'll be using an Illustrator file in Photoshop: Create the file using RGB colors. If necessary, you can convert the colors to RGB by choosing File > Document Color Mode > RGB Color.

When you're sharing artwork between the two programs, an important consideration is that Photoshop is raster-based and Illustrator is vector-based. Raster-based means that objects are described as pixels on a raster, or grid. Photoshop is better for working with organic shapes, such as those in photographs or paintings. Vector-based means that objects are mathematically described as points connected by straight or curved lines. Vector-based graphics generated in Illustrator have crisp, clear lines when scaled to any size. Because both programs can handle raster- and vector-based images, here are some things to think about when you use these programs together.

Raster versus vector

Before using Illustrator graphics in Photoshop, evaluate the artwork. Decide whether you want your shapes and type to have sharp, clean edges like the illustration below. If so, you will want to use the Copy and Paste method on page 323. When you paste the graphic, be sure to paste it as a path or shape layer to avoid rasterizing it. Then, when you print the graphic, see "Printing vector graphics from Photoshop" on page 321.

Vector artwork created in Illustrator

When you open an Illustrator file directly in Photoshop, you'll get the Rasterize dialog box. Minimize stair-stepping on curves by selecting the Anti-alias option. Change the color mode, if desired. Note that Photoshop will rasterize the entire Illustrator file into one image layer if you open it directly. To retain the file's layers, export the file from Illustrator (see "Export method" on page 321).

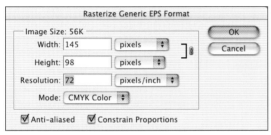

Photoshop's Rasterize dialog box

Depending on the file resolution, anti-aliasing can make the edges of objects appear fuzzy. Fuzziness with anti-aliasing is generally preferable to the stair-stepping appearance that occurs without it. Note in the illustration below that anti-aliasing does not improve the thick green line.

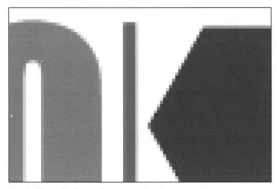

Anti-aliased edges after rasterization

On the other hand, if your artwork consists of vertical and horizontal lines and no curves, you can achieve better results without anti-aliasing. In this example, the green line looks

Opening multipage PDF documents

Illustrator's native format is PDF (Portable Document Format). PDF documents can contain multiple pages. Illustrator cannot save a multiple page document, but many other programs can export multipage PDF files. If you try to open one of these files with Photoshop, the PDF Page Selector dialog box will appear. Just click the page thumbnail you want, and only that page will open in Photoshop. The file will be flattened and may contain transparency because Photoshop will rasterize only objects on the page, not the white page itself.

sharp, but the curves and angles in the other shapes now have a jagged edge.

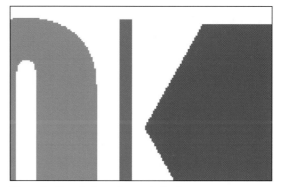

Nonanti-aliased edges after rasterization

Bringing Illustrator files into Photoshop

In Photoshop, you can choose from four ways to bring in Illustrator files: the Place command, Export and Open, Copy and Paste, or the Open command. If you want to be able to edit layers and text once the Illustrator file is opened in Photoshop, use the Export method to output the file from Illustrator. If you want to scale or transform the image to fit with an existing Photoshop file, use the Place method in Photoshop. The Copy and Paste method is best if you want to retain the outlines and use them as paths or shape layers in Photoshop.

Place method

1   In Photoshop, choose File > Place. Navigate to the Illustrator file you want to place, and click Place. Shift-drag the highlighted corners of the box to scale the image proportionally.

The advantage to this method is that you can easily transform the graphic before it is rasterized.

Placing an Illustrator graphic into a Photoshop file

2 When you have finished moving and transforming the graphic, press Return/Enter to complete the rasterization.

Another advantage to placing a graphic is that it is placed on its own layer with a transparent background.

Placed graphic with transparent background

Export method

1 In Illustrator, choose File > Export and select the Photoshop (PSD) format. Be sure to name the file differently than its Illustrator name. Click Export to open the Photoshop Options dialog box.

2 Select the resolution for the Photoshop file. If you want to keep the layers, select the Write Layers option. For smooth-

Printing vector graphics from Photoshop

You can print your type or shape layers so that they are resolution-independent while the other layers in your file maintain the same resolution. For example, if your file has a resolution of 72 ppi, any images you have in the file will print at 72 ppi, no matter what printer you use. But you can print the type and shape layers in the file at a higher resolution if you use a PostScript printer and follow these steps:

1 Choose File > Print With Preview.

2 Select Show More Options, and then choose Output from the pop-up menu.

3 Select Include Vector Data to print the type and shape layers as resolution-independent PostScript vectors instead of as resolution-dependent rasters.

edged graphics, select the Anti-alias option. If your file has text that you want to be able to edit in Photoshop, select the Editable Text option. Click OK.

Being able to edit text is one of the advantages of using this method.

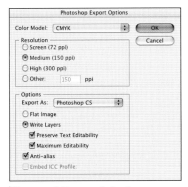

Illustrator's Export dialog box

3   Open the file in Photoshop.

The disadvantage to this method is that the file will be exactly the size of the graphics and no larger. If you want to add space around the edges of the graphic, choose Image > Canvas Size and increase the size of the canvas.

Layered Illustrator file opened in Photoshop

Copy and Paste method

1   Before copying the Illustrator graphic, choose Illustrator >
    Preferences > File Handling & Clipboard (Mac OS X)
    or Edit > Preferences > File Handling & Clipboard
    (Windows). To retain the paths in the file, select the AICB
    and Preserve Paths options. Click OK. Choose Edit > Copy
    to copy the selected artwork.

2   In Photoshop, choose Edit > Paste, and choose a Paste
    option:

    - Pixels to fill the graphic with the color specified in
      Illustrator; to transform it before rasterizing, press
      Return/Enter.

    - Path to paste the copy as a path in the Paths palette.

    - Shape Layer to fill the graphic with the current
      foreground color. If you chose Shape Layer, as in the
      following example, the size is the exact size it was in
      Illustrator; to change it, choose Edit > Free Transform.

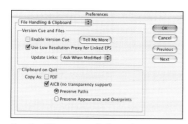

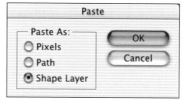

Set the Illustrator clipboard   *Choose an option for pasting*
preferences

3   Click OK to paste the graphic.

Illustrator graphic is pasted as a shape at its orginial size

Open method

Choose File > Open and open the Illustrator file. Choose the size, mode, and resolution, and click OK.

The file will open with all layers merged onto one layer. Be sure to rename the file when saving so as not to overwrite the original Illustrator file.

Bringing Photoshop files into Illustrator

There are four different ways to bring Photoshop files into Illustrator: the Place command, drag-and-drop, copy and paste, or the Open command. The drag-and-drop or copy and paste methods are less desirable because they convert the image to a 72-ppi, RGB image. However, you can copy paths created in Photoshop and paste them into an Illustrator file with no loss of image quality. Pasted paths, however, will always be filled and painted with None. If you open or place a layered Photoshop file, Illustrator can retain some of the layers—a nice feature if you want to be able to edit them in Illustrator.

Place command

In Illustrator, choose File > Place and turn on the Link option if you want to link the file; turn off the option if you want to embed the file.

The advantages to linking are that the file size stays small and you can update the image using the Links palette. The disadvantage is that you can't select or edit individual elements of the placed artwork.

Open command

In Illustrator, choose File > Open and select the Photoshop image. Illustrator creates an embedded image. Unfortunately, embedded images become part of the Illustrator file and increase its file size. The advantage to embedding is the ability to edit if you place a layered Photoshop file. You cannot edit a layered Photoshop file if it is linked.

Opening and placing layered Photoshop files

Choose File > Open or Place, and select a layered Photoshop file. If placing, deselect the Link option, and click Place. If opening, click Open to display the Photoshop Import Options dialog box. Choose whether to retain the layers:

- Select the Convert Photoshop Layers to Objects and Make Text Editable Where Possible option to maintain as many layers as possible. Illustrator will rasterize layers that contain layer effects, adjustment layers, certain layer modes, and clipping groups.

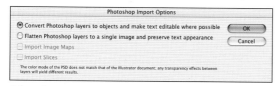

Select the Convert option to retain as many layers as possible

- Select the Flatten Photoshop Layers to a Single Image and Preserve Text Appearance option to flatten the file to a single layer.

Is the file linked or embedded?

The way to tell if you have linked or embedded artwork in your Illustrator file is to look at the Links palette. Linked files have no icon next to the file name. An embedded file will have a small square icon to the right of its name in the Links palette.

Linked file

Embedded file

Index

Credits

Author:	Luanne Seymour Cohen
Book Design/Production:	Jan Martí
Production Coordinator:	Lisa Brazieal
Cover Design:	Aren Howell
Executive Editor:	Becky Morgan
Copy Editor:	Judy Walthers von Alten
Indexer:	Judy Walthers von Alten
Technical Editor:	Sean Safreed

Photo and illustration credits

All photography and illustration were done by Luanne Seymour Cohen unless noted in the chart below. Italics indicate large sample illustrations.

Photographer/Artist	Page number(s)
Adobe Illustrator CD (Clip art files)	*116*, 117, 120, 211
Artbeats	305
Classic PIO Library	258
Albrecht Dürer	242
Michael Mabry	*108 (illustration)*
PhotoDisc	*108, 300, 162, 286-7*, 243, 249, 250 253, *274*, 275
Steven Ready	*58 (thistle), 66 (blossom), 134 (goat)*, 223, 295
Ultimate Symbol, Inc.	135, *172*, 192
Unknown	235

Colophon

This book was designed and produced using Adobe InDesign 2.0, Adobe Photoshop CS, and Adobe Illustrator CS. The Adobe Minion Pro and Myriad Pro typefaces are used throughout the book.

Training and inspiration from Adobe Press

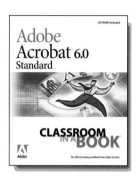

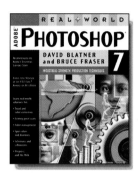

Classroom in a Book

The easiest, most comprehensive way to master Adobe software! *Classroom in a Book* is the bestselling series of practical software training workbooks. Developed with the support of product experts at Adobe Systems, these books offer complete, self-paced lessons designed to fit your busy schedule.

Each book includes a CD-ROM with customized files to guide you through the lessons and special projects.

Real World Series

Get industrial-strength production techniques from these comprehensive, "under-the-hood" reference books. Written by nationally recognized leaders in digital graphics, Web, and new media, these books offer timesaving tips, professional techniques, and detailed insight into how the software works. Covering basic through advanced skill levels, these books are ideal for print and Web graphics pros.

Idea Kits

The how-to books with a twist: Each features projects and templates that will jump-start your creativity, jog your imagination, and help you make the most of your Adobe software—fast! All the files you'll need are included on the accompanying disk, ready to be customized with your own artwork. You'll get fast, beautiful results without the learning curve.

Other Classics

Adobe Press books are the best way to go beyond the basics of your favorite Adobe application. Gain valuable insight and inspiration from well-known artists and respected instructors. Titles such as *The Complete Manual of Typography*, *Adobe Master Class: Design Invitational*, *Creating Acrobat Forms*, *Adobe Photoshop Web Design*, and *Photoshop One-Click Wow!* will put you on the fast track to mastery in no time.

The fastest, easiest, most comprehensive way to master Adobe Software

Visit www.adobepress.com for these titles and more!